Dear

Prof Jitendra V Singh,

Asean needs

a Professor like you

and a Company like NTU/NBS

to be the / hub of Asia

linking India and China

in Business Knowledge Dynamics,

MarkPlus Inc Jakarta, -

19 May 08

Hermawan Kartajaya.

Think ASEAN!

Rethinking Marketing
toward ASEAN Community 2015

Philip Kotler
Hermawan Kartajaya
Hooi Den Huan

Singapore • Boston • Burr Ridge, IL • Dubuque, IA • Madison, WI • New York • San Francisco
St. Louis • Bangkok • Kuala Lumpur • Lisbon • London • Madrid • Mexico City
Milan • Montreal • New Delhi • Seoul • Sydney • Taipei • Toronto

The *McGraw·Hill* Companies

Think ASEAN!
Rethinking Marketing toward ASEAN Community 2015

 **Education**

Cover design by Norman Illyas Manorbang, Brand Credence, MarkPlus, Inc

1 2 3 4 5 6 7 8 9 10 CTF SLP 20 10 09 08 07

When ordering this title, use ISBN 978-007-125405-2 or MHID 007-125405-6

Printed in Singapore

Foreword I

As businesses expand in the ASEAN region, companies must focus on getting their marketing strategies right. They must ensure that their sales pitches are heard above the din of competition. They must learn how to engage increasingly savvy, empowered, and well-informed customers. They must know their customers and connect with them. Marketers must thoroughly understand local, cultural, demographic, and psychological characteristics and use them to create opportunities to be truly relevant. They must think ASEAN!

Today's leading brands are personalities in their own right and are well known in their respective societies and cultures, just as great leaders, sports or movie celebrities, and even cartoon characters. Millions of people relate to brand personalities in the same way as they do to human personalities. Thus, the secret to successful branding is to influence the way in which people perceive the company or product. Brands influence buying decisions by combing the physical and emotional elements that appeal to customers who are living, or would like to live, a certain lifestyle; or who are expressing themselves to others by demonstrating that they have achieved something or are different. Additionally, brands give consumers the means to make choices and judgments. Relying on chosen brands can guarantee standards of quality and service, reducing the risk of failure in purchase. Branding success is therefore dependent on understanding what the customer is looking for. In the increasingly competitive marketplace, brands can be crucial to customer loyalty and longer-term survival and growth.

Even countries must engage in marketing and branding for a variety of reasons: from attracting investments and trade promotion to garnering developmental aid. Indeed, the ASEAN region must leverage on its comparative and competitive advantages to remain relevant and prosperous in an interconnected world dominated by preferential regional trading blocs. The process of packaging and promoting ASEAN's unique qualities to its citizenry and the world at large is a multidimensional challenge, requiring the cooperation and creativity of governments, businesses, and civil society organizations, within and outside ASEAN.

These days, compelling marketing is pertinent marketing. Marketing relevancy takes effort and imagination but the rewards are immense as the companies highlighted in *Think ASEAN!* illustrate. They are testimony to the fact that customers will listen if marketers take time to be relevant. *Think ASEAN!* provides valuable insights into how ASEAN and multinational corporations have successfully worked their marketing magic in the region. I have no doubt that *Think ASEAN!* will serve as a useful reference for those planning to tap, or are already tapping, into ASEAN's vast integrated market of more than 500 million people.

Ong Keng Yong
Secretary-General, ASEAN

Foreword II

The economies of ASEAN are at a crucial stage of their development as they adjust to progressive trade liberalization and market opening, both within the region and in the world at large. ASEAN countries, once among the leaders in the developing world in openness and economic growth, now encounter increased competition for their exports to world markets. They also face intensified competition for domestic as well as foreign investments, and in their own domestic markets, particularly from their large and rapidly growing neighbors China and India.

Individual ASEAN economies remain small and fragmented by global standards. This makes them both less cost-competitive in production in the many sectors where economies of scale are significant, and less attractive locations for market-oriented investments, particularly given their added heterogeneity in terms of income levels, languages, and cultures. At the same time, the region's favorable natural resource endowment, relatively stable macroeconomic and political environment, large collective population, and potentially complementary country comparative advantages offer compensating attractions and opportunities for both local and international business.

Both ASEAN's competitive economic weaknesses and strengths call for progress toward an integrated regional market, to offset size limitations on the one hand, and to make the most of relative regional advantages, on the other. This is a necessarily long-term project at the inter-governmental policy level. But the private business sector which accounts for most of ASEAN's GDP cannot and should not wait till an integrated single market is created by government policy before developing and implementing its own regional business strategies. Rather, private business actions can and should initiate a process of market-led regional integration that is likely to be not just quicker, but also more efficient, as a result.

It is in this context that I consider this book to be both timely and valuable. The authors take a bold and creative, yet rigorous and systematic, approach to preparing for, operating in, and profiting from an integrated regional market before it has fully emerged. Their analysis and suggestions are useful both for national companies seeking to "go regional" as part of a strategy of fending off intensified home-market competition from other regional as well as global players, and for non-ASEAN multinationals seeking to enhance their global footprints with a share of the regional market.

Regional economic integration in an increasingly globally integrated world is a challenge, but one that can be successfully met if individual companies step up to meet this challenge. This forward-looking and imaginative, yet highly practical book will help them to do so, with its focus on delivering global value by employing regional strategies and local tactics.

Linda Lim
Professor of Corporate Strategy and International Business
Director, Center for Southeast Asian Studies
University of Michigan, Ann Arbor, US

Preface

Have you noticed an interesting phenomenon recently in Southeast Asia? Let us give you some clues.

BreadTalk, the Singapore-based bakery, is spreading its bread boutique to Jakarta, Malaysia, and the Philippines. AirAsia, the Malaysia-based low-cost carrier, is spreading its wings to Thailand with its Thai AirAsia and to Indonesia with its Indonesia AirAsia. Black Canyon, the Thailand-based coffee shop, is dispersing its unique coffee flavors in Indonesia, Singapore, and Malaysia.

Moreover, you can see Es Teller 77, one of Indonesia's largest restaurant chains, in Orchard Road, Singapore. Pho24, the famous noodle restaurant chain in Vietnam, is now open in Indonesia. You can also see San Miguel beer, which originates in the Philippines, now widely available across and even beyond the region.

What is happening?

The answer is simple: Regionalization is happening in Southeast Asia! The Association of Southeast Asian Nations (ASEAN) is no longer just an association of neighboring countries. It is becoming one integrated market that possesses great potential. The market is not mature so there is room for aggressive growth. Companies are eyeing this market and have started to go regional.

The development of Asia after the Asian financial crisis has been tremendous. On the whole, not only are Asian countries performing a great comeback, but they are also emerging as the new powerhouse of the world. Economically, China in particular is growing at a very fast pace. It has become the new manufacturing hub of the world. China can make anything and everything cheaper than other countries. The 1.3 billion population, as one huge market, adds to the excitement it creates. It is even dubbed the world's new superpower. India is another superpower. It, however, has chosen to be the service hub of the world. The Indian outsourcing service has changed how business is done today, especially in the IT and telecommunication sectors.

Both new world superpowers have become Asia's major business attraction at this moment. However, through this book, we would like to introduce you to a new emerging market as an alternative: ASEAN. This market may not be as attractive as the superpowers, but as we stated earlier, the market possesses great potential that should not be missed.

For those who are from local companies in ASEAN, we would like to encourage you to capture this opportunity because it is the most feasible market to target. China and India are very promising markets because of the low cost of resources and the large population bases. Nevertheless, they are at times far too competitive to enter. ASEAN, on the other hand, may offer an alternative viable market. The emergence of ASEAN as one entity has one aggregate potential—both as a production base and as a target market. Its low-cost structure—although not as low as China's—and 600 million population plus the closer geographic distance make ASEAN an attractive alternative. Instead of just chasing after the highly competitive and relatively more distant markets of China and India, you should look to ASEAN markets, especially if you have operations in Southeast Asia.

The Miracle of ASEAN Is Back!!!

There is no doubt that the Asian crisis in mid-1997 has had a significant impact on ASEAN member countries. The power of ASEAN itself as one entity to face the crisis was being questioned at the time. However, as the crisis is over, each of the ASEAN countries is regaining its dignity and bringing back the miracle of the region through more efforts, individually and collectively. These efforts have now shown some remarkable achievements in making ASEAN one of the most important regions within the Asia Pacific.

As one entity, ASEAN also launched several joint efforts to support each country's individual efforts. One of the efforts is by raising the ambitious vision of becoming one community: ASEAN Community 2015. ASEAN member countries have agreed in principle to speed up efforts to create a single market by 2015, five years ahead of schedule.[1] The ASEAN Community will lean on three pillars: ASEAN Security Community, ASEAN Economic Community, and ASEAN Socio-Cultural Community to create a peaceful, prosperous, and people-centric ASEAN. This common vision of becoming one community has made ASEAN countries work hand in hand to achieve its goals.

At the corporate level, this emerging community has created a paradox in the business world. A progressively more unified and borderless ASEAN will pose greater business challenges to the local players in the region. They are not only competing with the other local players, but also with competitors from neighboring countries and multinationals penetrating their home market. However, this business challenge also comes along with tremendous marketing opportunity. The huge market of ASEAN can be more attractive than the limited home market. Local players have started to eye this opportunity. Large multinationals have even started building regional production bases for the ASEAN market. The increasingly dynamic and tangible ASEAN as a regional production base and as one single market shows that ASEAN Community 2015 is not merely a dream.

This fact also supports the argument that regionalization is the new emerging trend that is even more important than globalization. Globalization is no longer valid, especially for large multinationals. They have been expanding their businesses globally to take advantage of globalization. It is a done deal for them. Now, it is time for regionalization. It is time for them to focus on specific regions. On the other hand, local companies see globalization as something that is too abstract in scope. That is why they are also aiming at the regional market.

ASEAN, as one market, possesses the quality of being targeted by both multinationals focusing on ASEAN and locals going regional.

---

[1] John Burton, "ASEAN Aims for Single Market by 2015," the *Financial Times*, August 22, 2006.

Multinationals think of ASEAN as the potential unsaturated market. On the other hand, locals seeking to expand, think of ASEAN as the real tangible market to go after since other countries and regions in the Asia Pacific may be too distant for them. That is why ASEAN has now become one of Asia's major attractions, besides China and India, for business people around the globe.

Think ASEAN!

One question arises: How can the ASEAN market be captured? In this book, we try to answer this one question.

We argue that both multinational corporations and local companies that seek entry into the ASEAN market will require regional marketing. Specifically, they will need ASEAN Marketing approaches. This is where the Philip Kotler Center for ASEAN Marketing, as a non-profit organization, fits in—to promote to the ASEAN marketers that ASEAN marketing may be a more relevant tool than just local or global marketing.

This book, which is the first publication of the Philip Kotler Center for ASEAN Marketing, tries to explore how companies should think of ASEAN as one borderless market that requires different marketing strategies to capture. It offers fresh perspectives to marketers all over the region about the upcoming trends of regionalization that can cause significant changes in future marketing activities. It argues that ASEAN marketers should not only be concerned about their local or global but also their regional marketing activities.

The Executive Summary explores why you will need ASEAN Vision and Local Action to engage the regional market. Part I describes the landscape of ASEAN and explains clearly why we need ASEAN Marketing. Parts II and III discuss companies that have been very successful in implementing ASEAN Marketing—Part II contains short cases of companies in ASEAN that explore their core marketing strategies while Part III contains comprehensive cases that explore the detailed marketing strategies of selected companies in ASEAN.

By reading this book, we hope that you will have a comprehensive understanding of what kind of strategy and tactic to apply when dealing with the ASEAN market. We certainly hope that you are also inspired to bring your company to the region and begin to THINK ASEAN!

Philip Kotler
Hermawan Kartajaya
Hooi Den Huan

Acknowledgments

We would like to thank several people who have been invaluable in helping us complete this book: Joan Li Shiwei, Joan Yap, Grace Sai, Tran Hoang, Huynh Phuoc Nghia, and in particular, Iwan Setiawan and Waizly Darwin.

We appreciate very much the support and assistance from McGraw-Hill and its editorial team who have been very helpful, especially Jerene Tan, Wati Seladin, Pauline Chua, and Irene Yeow.

Contents

Foreword I   *iii*

Foreword II   *v*

Preface   *vii*

Acknowledgments   *xii*

Executive Summary: Forget the World, Think ASEAN,
Act Local   *1*

Part I   ASEAN from the Top   5

Chapter 1   Digital Technology in ASEAN   *11*

Chapter 2   Impact of Globalization on ASEAN   *25*

Chapter 3   The Future Market of ASEAN   *42*

Chapter 4   Compete for ASEAN Customers   *66*

Part II   Lessons from ASEAN Marketing Companies   83

Chapter 5   Watch out for the Local Champions   *85*

Bengawan Solo   *86*

Dji Sam Soe   *90*

Goldilocks   *94*

MBF Cards   *97*

Bangkok Hospital   *101*

Number One Tonic Drink in Vietnam   *105*

Chapter 6   Learn from the Locals Going ASEAN   *113*

Extra Joss   *113*

Royal Selangor   *117*

San Miguel   *120*

Eu Yan Sang   *124*

Black Canyon   *128*

Chapter 7   Be Inspired by Multinationals Focusing on
              ASEAN   *133*
     3M   *134*
     Kinokuniya   *139*
     Samsung   *143*

Part III   ASEAN Marketing in Practice   *149*

Chapter 8   ASEAN Vision, Local Action   *151*
     Air Asia   *152*
     BreadTalk   *159*
     Kijang   *164*
Chapter 9   Global Value, ASEAN Strategy, Local Tactic   *173*
     Hewlett-Packard   *176*
     Yamaha   *179*

Index   *187*

Executive Summary

Forget the World, Think ASEAN, Act Local

In the last 20 years, *globalization* has been the most discussed topic among heads of states, policy makers, business leaders, and generally anyone whose life and work has been affected one way or another by this phenomenon. But globalization is not new. The earliest form of globalization began about 3,000 years ago when the sea-faring Phoenician traders built trading posts around the Mediterranean region. Their commercial activities served the great Egyptian and Babylonian civilizations and thus created a prosperous and powerful era for the Phoenicia people of that time.

Over centuries, trading of goods and services between countries has evolved dramatically with new discoveries and experiences. Technology, whether it is the invention of the wheel, steam engine, or computer, plays a crucial role in the search for and the achievements of improved living conditions, wealth, power, and knowledge. It is evident that technology is the main driver and globalization the key enabler of the accelerated economic growth throughout the agricultural, industrial, and digital revolutions.

Whether one likes it or not, globalization is the inevitable and irreversible process which serves a primary function in the world system economically, politically, socially, and technologically. The winners in globalization are not confined to the rich developed countries. The winners are those who adopt open-market policies to exploit the flow of capital and technologies to be globally integrated in order to conduct cross-border trade competitively. In recent years, India and China have benefited from rapid growth and poverty reduction as a result of globalization. On the other hand, early advocates of globalization are experiencing increasing unemployment as jobs are being transferred to lower-cost countries.

However, globalization is not a single process or a "one size fits all" solution. The World Trade Organization (WTO) had aimed to ensure a smooth global commercial environment where trade flows freely and predictably through a multilateral system for its member nations. This motion was challenged at the third WTO ministerial conference in Seattle, US in 1999, with massive protests drawing worldwide attention and ending the talks in failure. At the heart of the demonstrations was the frustration from those who feared the prospect of being sidelined through a multilateral system where trade treaties were biased toward wealthy nations and multinational companies. These parties began to look for more practical and less compromising options to integrate globally by means of regionalization and regional trade agreements.

An impetus for greater regionalization is seen as neighboring countries polarized to work around the issues in a global framework in order to stay globalized. Another motivation for regionalization is that smaller countries tend to have less bargaining power and room for concessions than the larger trading countries, resulting in huge trade-offs and lower benefits. For ASEAN countries, there is yet a much more compelling reason for regionalization, that is, the need to be independent, competitive, and complementary in the light of new high-growth economies around the region.

The relationship among the Asian countries has been socially, politically, and economically driven. The economic driver is best explained by the "flying geese," a term first coined by Japanese scholar Kaname Akamatsu in the 1930s and revisited in his 1961 publication *A Theory of Unbalanced Growth in the World Economy*. It explains the flying geese formation in the shape of an inverted "V" as a depiction that competitiveness first improves and then deteriorates over time as countries progress. Industries will be forced to · shift from more advanced (expensive) countries to less developed countries where costs are lower. The flying geese model demonstrates the economic dynamics from the expansion of Japan as the "lead goose" to the newly industrialized economies (NIEs) and further to Southeast Asia, China, and South Asia.

Unfortunately the performing countries of the 1980s Asian miracle were hit by one crisis after another beginning with Japan's banking collapse in the early 1990s and ending in the Asian financial crisis in 1997. This put an end to the flying geese formation. In recent years, Asia's geopolitical landscape has changed considerably, influenced mainly by the emerging economic superpowers China and India.

A new regionalism is forming in Asia with squadrons of flying geese taking shape on the business horizon. Japan, China, and South Korea individually have the economic, financial, and technological might to integrate globally. In the Indian sub-continent, the eight-nation South Asian Association for Regional Cooperation (SAARC) was established in 1985. SAARC, led by India and Pakistan, aims to cooperate socially and economically for a population of 1.4 billion people. In Southeast Asia, the ten-nation Association of Southeast Asian Nations (ASEAN), established in 1967, is fast becoming an active regional trading bloc.

For years, ASEAN's agenda has been politically- and security-oriented. The industrialization and globalization efforts of the founding members—Indonesia, Malaysia, the Philippines, Singapore, and Thailand—have turned ASEAN toward more economic objectives, priming it toward a single community, market, and production base. Thus, when we say "forget the world, think regional, act local," we mean to draw your attention back to this region and refocus in an area that you might have the greatest comparative advantage to integrate globally. Do not make the mistake that the first step to globalization is to open offices all over the world. Globalization is not about physical locations in various parts of the world.

Globalization is about how we integrate with the global economy by attracting investments and technologies and in turn using capital and technologies to produce goods and services at the most competitive prices while providing the highest value to our local, regional, and global customers. With open economies, the best way to integrate globally is to tap local and regional resources to reach out to the world. Build a stronghold in the domestic market and in this region first. Develop a sturdy network by taking advantage of regional trade arrangements and collective size. Understand what regional customers want and create quality products and services that differentiate us from our competitors.

There will always be changes and the rate of change will continue to increase. The world's first search engine was launched only seven years ago yet "google" is now being used as a verb in daily communications. A search on the Internet for the word "world" yields over six billion results in 0.2 seconds. That is the speed and scope of our world today—fast, efficient, and available at our fingertips. How do businesses keep pace with developments, stay focused, maintain growth, remain competitive, and integrate themselves into the global markets? The answer lies in regionalization.

Think ASEAN! is a book written for business people and marketers to understand the forces of change and the impact of globalization and regionalization on future markets. It highlights the opportunities in ASEAN today and shares models of enterprising and innovative companies who have established themselves successfully in this region.

Forget the world, think ASEAN now!

Part I

ASEAN from the Top

ASEAN is an organization as well as a community of countries made up of multiracial, multilanguage, and multireligion societies linked by geographical proximity and historical ties. Contemporary ASEAN cities give little hint of their tumultuous past. Skyscrapers now stand in old districts that were once damaged by war and neglect. Spread over an area of 4,480,000 km^2 with a population of more than 540 million indigenous people, immigrants, and scions of inter-marriages, ASEAN is a classic model of social and cultural integration. As a region, it offers a rich diversity of talents, traditions, resources, and opportunities. Though integrated, the ASEAN countries are markedly different in what each can offer one another and collectively as a group.

In this first part of the book we will discuss the changing business landscape driven by inherent and external forces, the factors influencing these forces, the challenges facing the region, and the opportunities to be exploited. Many of the changes are not new but the main variables today are the speed of change due to technological advances, the adoption rate as a result of globalization, and the reaction to these changes from a new breed of well-informed global customers. Businesses have to move from being product-centric to being customer-centric. Fast-moving consumer goods (FMCG) which used to refer to products with rapid shelf turnover such as soft drinks and toiletries, may soon include mobile technologies such as mobile phones.

Globalization with all good intentions has its side effects. Governments and business leaders are battling with policies and strategies to reform and restructure their existing organizations to position themselves for the global economies. Old rules of doing business will have to morph to stay relevant and competitive in global markets. There will be sacrifices and compromises, winners and losers, but no one in the quest for progress and prosperity would want to be left behind.

In our book *Rethinking Marketing: Sustainable Market-ing Enterprise in Asia*, we analyze the business landscape by using the "4C Diamond" sub-model (see Figure A). Change is the dynamic factor that determines the external macroeconomic environment which in turn influences an organization's strategy formulation.

The forces of change consist of five elements—technology, political-legal, social-cultural, economy, and market (see Figure B). Technology is the primary force of change that directly impacts on the way we live and work. It influences political and legal systems, economic development, and social-cultural standards. These changes indirectly create new markets and retire old ones. The interaction among the forces gives rise to three major "streams."

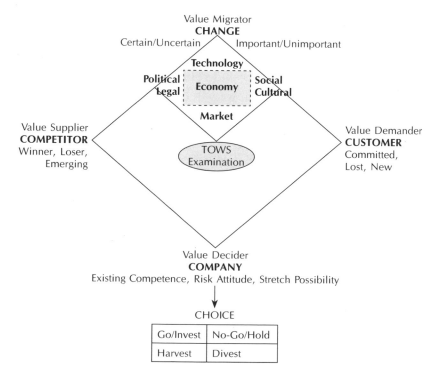

Figure A   The 4C Diamond sub-model

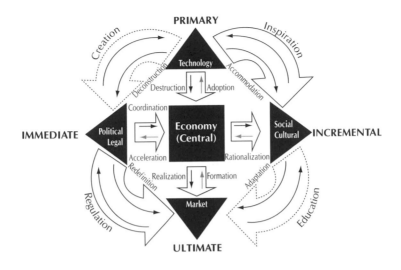

Figure B   The forces of change in the business landscape

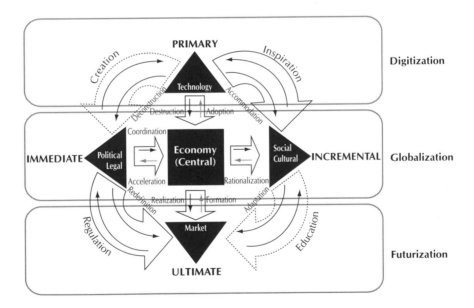

Figure C   The horizontal stream of change

The first or "horizontal" stream shows the cause and effect of change (see Figure C). Technology today enables the digitization of information which facilitates the widespread dissemination of information, ideas, and public opinion. The worldwide movement of goods, services, resources, and cultures is accelerated by technology as open economies integrate into the global marketplace. Improved living conditions, spending patterns, and consumers' sophistication generate new market trends which lead to research and innovation of better future products and services.

The second or "vertical" stream demonstrates the flow for change that will be constructive and beneficial to all (see Figure D). Public policies and political goals must be designed to ensure peace and stability. In open economies, regional cooperation is essential to promote development and growth. Progress and prosperity in a region will enhance the general well-being of everyone.

The third or "S" stream explains the "time and impact" significance of change in a globalized world (see Figure E). For decades, the world has benefited and advanced tremendously with the advent of technology. The revelation of a borderless and timeless world shifts

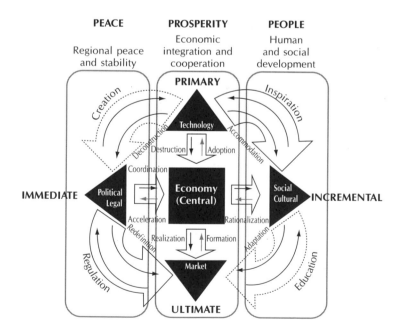

Figure D   The vertical stream of change

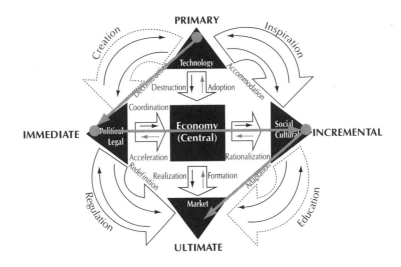

Figure E   The S stream of change

the seat of power from those who have to those who know. In his book *The World Is Flat* Thomas L. Friedman wrote that "globalization has brought people and cultures together like never before." His concept of a flat world is derived from the leveling of the world's economic playing field by technological forces and the irrelevance of time and space as a result. Technology will be agents of change in politics which in turn drive economies, impact societies, and develop markets.

Chapter 1 explores the digitization of the world and how digital technology serves to bring information and places to people easily and affordably. The world has become smaller and larger at the same time—smaller in terms of virtual distances and time needed to do things, and larger in terms of markets and choices.

Chapter 2 explains the impact of globalization on ASEAN by tracing the effects of market liberalization and the level of exposure of open economies to global changes. Post-crisis ASEAN faces new competition from globalization giants China and India, but at the same time benefits from the opportunities of increasing wealth around the region.

Chapter 3 looks at ASEAN as an organization, a community, and a region. To ensure continuous growth in an ever-changing market, businesses must adopt a sustainable growth philosophy. Marketing must come from an outside-in approach in order to spot the correct market trends and customer demands.

Chapter 4 concludes Part I by targeting the heart of every business—how to win customers and fight competition. An organization identified as one with integrity, credibility, and value will continue to keep its customers and be profitable. Positioning, differentiation, and branding are the three focal points in building a successful organization.

chapter 1

Digital Technology in ASEAN

The globalization of the economy and today's breathtaking technological advances have brought a critical mass of the world's people closer together.[1]

Roldolfo C. Severino and Jose Jesus F. Roces

A decade ago, real-time market information was available only to closed user groups connected to private computer networks. The infrastructure to deliver the information and maintain the host systems was expensive and mostly proprietary. When the Internet arrived in the early 1990s, conservative brick-and-mortar businesses were apprehensive, cynical, and unwilling to accept its openness and interconnectivity. Disregarded as a technologist's plaything, the Internet was clearly a threat to traditional ways of operations, management, and control of information and resources. However, the incessant adoption of inter-networking fueled the explosive growth of a web-based, supply-driven, service-oriented, content-rich, borderless, and timeless paradigm, dragging its critics kicking and fussing into the new online dimension.

Though the Internet has linked the world and revolutionized computing networking, its adoption would not have been as widespread if not for the pervasive digitization of data, image, and voice. Digital technology transforms the way we use information and changes our personal, social, economic, and political environments. In a mere ten years, new work patterns and lifestyles have been

---

[1] Rodolfo Severino and Jose Jesus Roces, "The Many Facets of Regional Economic Integration: Impact and Implications for ASEAN," *Nanyang Business Review*, Vol. 1, No. 2, July–December 2002.

created which in turn change conventional organizational structures, processes, and policies. From consumer products such as cameras and digital music players to tagging devices using radio frequency identification (RFID), digital technology paves the way for multidisciplinary and diversified technologies. In the near future, the old telly may disappear completely when Internet Protocol Television (IPTV) enables video to be distributed over broadband and cellular networks to the same PC or mobile phone that you use to prepare your business presentations, to email, and to engage in web meetings. It is no wonder that one of the world's largest IT corporations, Hewlett-Packard, will include TV in their strategic consumer business.

In this chapter we will discuss digital technology in ASEAN, the significance of the digital divide, technology as a driving force behind economic development, and what ASEAN countries are doing to harness technology for the benefits of the region.

Digital Revolution—Hype or Reality?

From the earliest inventions and discoveries, technology has been the key driver of economic development, social advancement, and political power. Be it the invention of the wheel, the steam engine, or the computer, technology has contributed to changes in work organization, productivity, economic growth, national security, and quality of life. With the introduction of new technologies, there have always been apprehension and skepticism that machines will replace mankind and incumbent processes. This is both wrong and right. Technology in itself could not replace mankind but merely redefines jobs and shifts the manual and repetitive work from a human to a machine. At the same time, technology opens up new channels for communication, transaction, and entertainment. Video did not kill the radio star as it was feared (and sung about in a hit song) when videotape recording made its debut in the late 1970s. Digitizing books has not caused the sale of books to drop; instead it has made searching easier for the buyer and has helped with the purchasing process.

The only thing that digital technology has clearly replaced is analog systems. Analog systems are based on physical attributes such as frequency, magnitudes, and phases. The key limitation of analog data is its propensity to drift from the original and therefore cause error in the output information. Digital is not infinitely adjustable and only has one of two unambiguous states, that is, either a 1 or a 0. Digital information has what is known as the "D4 advantage"—Digital Data Doesn't Degrade. Information on computer systems which are based on digital data never changes or becomes distorted over time or in transmission over long distances. This is the key feature that makes it possible to construct the very complex software systems that run the Internet so that a web site does not degrade and become fuzzy or garbled.

While the technologies of past civilizations and pre-war economies revolved mainly around the production of goods and services as in the agricultural and industrial eras, the technology of our time is mostly information-based in the form of digital data, processes, storage, communications, and displays. Information technology (IT) has evolved from pulse-code modulation, vacuum tubes, and germanium transistors, to integrated circuit chips, microprocessors, and triple-play "infotainment" devices. Beginning with simple, limited, specialized systems that use discrete binary numbers for input and processing, IT has advanced to complex high-performance interactive devices and gadgets so user-friendly even some three-year-olds can handle them. More importantly, IT has become an integral part of urban living from microwave ovens to personal digital assistants (PDAs).

Digital technology has enabled faster and less costly product innovation, manufacturing process redesign, and shorter product lifecycles due to more efficient access to marketing data and rapid prototyping. Henry Ford's Model T automobile was designed and built for the masses where 15 million of the same black model were sold over 19 years. This will never be acceptable today. Modern manufacturing has made possible custom-designed products to the masses at even lower prices such as the mobile phone market where new models with different functionalities and pricing for different market segments are launched almost every month—complete with a full range of colors and trimmings. Mass customization has become a reality.

Economies that embrace technologies to produce faster and cheaper will benefit because of the ability to increase market share and penetrate into new markets (see Figure 1.1). Technology is a key growth driver with its ability to accelerate production and innovation, which in turn speeds up economic progress. Markets will get larger when better and cheaper products are made available. Expanded markets provide motivation and justification for research and development of improved future products. Vibrant industries support employment, enhance living standards, raise income levels, and stimulate economic growth.

The expansion of markets is most visible in today's convergence in information and communication technologies (ICT). The effects of globalization and the amalgamation of ICT industries augment the push for interoperability, open standards, competition, and transparency of information and connectivity. After a series of false starts and inadequate mobile networks and equipment, third-generation (3G) technology is finally making its mark in "triple play" presentation of voice data (telephone call) and non-voice data (downloadable information, email, and instant messaging). ICT convergence has led to myriad possibilities for innovative applications and immense opportunities for bridging the *digital divide* between those who have and those who have not.

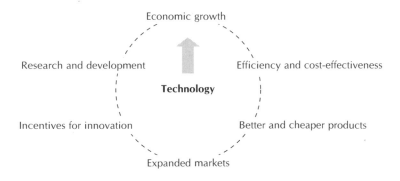

Figure 1.1   The impact of technology on economic growth

Digital Challenges and Opportunities

In November 2000, ASEAN entered into the e-ASEAN Framework Agreement to facilitate the establishment of the ASEAN Information Infrastructure (AII) and collectively promote the growth of e-services and e-commerce in business, society, and government. This initiative encompasses interconnectivity and technical interoperability among telecommunication systems and equipment in the region. The key areas of focus are

- Fostering favorable legal and policy environment for the development and use of ICT.
- Liberalization of trade in ICT products and services.
- Promotion of investments in the production and provision of ICT products and services.

The impetus for e-ASEAN is due to the explosive growth of ICT worldwide and the speed of growth has inadvertently made it harder for less developed countries to catch up with rapid changes. Within countries, the digital divide exists between cities and rural areas where electricity may not even be available, let alone PCs or the Internet. It is therefore important for ASEAN to narrow the gap so that all countries in the region can take advantage of the ICT advancement and integrate globally as a single competitive trading bloc. In the 2005 publication of Orbicom, the International Network of UNESCO Chairs in Communications, it is reported that the ASEAN digital divide is clearly represented by the spread between low ICT-enabled countries such as Myanmar and Laos and high ICT-enabled countries such as Singapore. Orbicom defines the degree of a country's "ICT-ization" or the "infostate" as the aggregation of the ICT infrastructure, skills, uptake, and intensity of use. From the report, we have extracted the data for ASEAN (see Table 1.1) and highlighted the following key observations:

- Infostate for all countries increased from 1995 to 2003 (at least by 127%).
- Countries with the lowest infostate experienced the highest growth rates (Cambodia, Laos, Myanmar, and Vietnam).

Table 1.1   Evolution of infostate in ASEAN countries

	1995	2003	ICT Growth
Brunei	50.5	114.5	127%
Cambodia	2.8	16.9	504%
Indonesia	12.8	44.6	248%
Laos	2.9	22.7	683%
Malaysia	30.6	110.9	262%
Myanmar	1.4	10.7	664%
Philippines	16.5	60.5	267%
Thailand	24.2	78.5	224%
Singapore	87.3	225.7	159%
Vietnam	2.7	37	1,270%
Digital divide	85.9	215	

Source: "From the Digital Divide to Digital Opportunities," Orbicom 2005.

- The digital divide between the highest and lowest infostates is widening (Singapore and Myanmar: 85.9 in 1995 and 215 in 2003).

ICT infrastructure is the major contributor to the overall digital divide. It includes IT and telecommunications facilities; fixed-line and mobile phone networks; all computer hardware and software; and data that supports, manages, and houses the input, processing, storage, distribution, and output of information in the form of digital data, digitized voice and images, and streamed video. Digitization plays a big part in ICT growth because digitized information is easier to manage and cheaper to handle. This promotes the development of new applications and proliferation of hardware and software that combine the advantages of mobile computing power, broadband wireless communications, high-definition displays, and lightweight materials.

The challenges and opportunities in ASEAN vary from one country to another and from one industry to another. Networking the whole country does not demand as much resources for small nation states like Brunei and Singapore as compared to Indonesia or the Philippines where analog telephone lines still exist. With regard to the more "ICT-able" industries, the banking sector is better positioned to adopt and implement ICT services because of its computerization background than say, the mining or agricultural industries. The positive note arising from these disparities is that growth potential in areas that have low ICT density and usage or have not been ICT-ized is remarkably huge. Businesses involved in ICT infrastructural projects, training, and professional services will be in high demand.

This does not mean that the countries with higher infostates have fewer opportunities. Technology breeds innovation and innovation leads to progress and more opportunities. That "everything that can be invented has been invented" as quoted in 1899 by the commissioner of the US Office of Patents has been proven wrong for the past 100 years. Inventions and discoveries will continue as long as there are new desires. Technology is an accumulation of building blocks that apply and enhance the next generation of goods and services. The opportunities for countries with high infostates are therefore to build on the current technologies to produce better products with improved cost efficiency for future consumers.

Opportunities and challenges are interconnected. To harvest the fruits of success, it is necessary to toil the ground first. Because the opportunities for different countries and industries are not the same, the challenges will also be different. In general, the basic ICT foundation must be in place before engaging in any ICT or ICT-related activities. A good analogy is building roads and training drivers before cars can populate a country. The information highway and the skilled workers must be present before ICT projects and jobs can be created and economic growth realized.

For low infostate economies in Cambodia, Laos, and Myanmar, the challenge is to lay the necessary foundation for opportunities in ICT development. In parallel to establishing the ICT infrastructure, literacy and skill levels must be increased through national education and special training for ICT-related work. Access to ICT must also be made affordable for the majority of people and businesses. It is very difficult for an ordinary Laotian, Cambodian, or Myanmese to afford a US$1,000 PC on an average monthly income of US$160, as compared to a Singaporean earning an average of US$2,000 per month. The greatest challenge for low infostate countries is financing ICT development either through foreign direct investments, overseas development assistance, bilateral funding, or loans. The opportunities are abundant for providers of fixed lines, mobile networks, hosts, consumer equipment, business systems, professional services, training, consultancy, and project management.

Brunei, Malaysia, Thailand, Indonesia, the Philippines, and Vietnam—countries that have intermediate to moderate infostate economies—started ICT initiatives from as early as 1990. PC literacy and adequacy is, compared with other developing countries, higher than India for all the six countries and higher than China for all except Indonesia. These countries have well-established ICT infrastructures in the major cities, rudimentary facilities in suburban towns, and virtually non-existent basic telecommunications in remote rural areas. Normalizing the ICT status of the outlying towns and industries with the cities is the greatest challenge for these geographically and demographically large countries. Efforts to update and upgrade the existing infrastructures to provide for an expanded user base will produce economies of scale for these countries, thereby bringing down ICT costs. With the cost of ownership lowered for the consumers and as businesses' adoption of technology increases, work efficiency and productivity will improve which then drives the general economy. Opportunities in providing new value-added services with product bundling incentives, competitive subscriptions, and transaction costs could transform marginal ICT projects into rewarding mainstream businesses.

The main challenge for high infostate Singapore is sustaining growth in a saturated and advanced market. Innovation is crucial here and different aspects of ICT deployment must be explored to seek new markets. Research and development plays an important role in mapping out future technologies and applications, instituting fresh technology disciplines, and investing in leading-edge intellectual development.

The ICT rage is here and now. Digital applications, services, and equipment are growing at breakneck speeds and continue to affect our lives and economies one way or another—in communications, banking, trade processing, inventory control, entertainment, production management, law enforcement, healthcare, weather forecasting—the list goes on. The preparedness to participate in ICT growth is the key to survival. The gap in the digital divide is expected to widen. Those who are not ready will be marginalized and stay in the low end of the digital divide. Countries with weak ICT strategies will experience slower economic development as they are unable to respond faster, negotiate better, and identify trends more accurately. In today's digital world ICT growth relates directly to economic growth.

ICT Strategies

Recognizing the importance of ICT, the relationship between ICT and economic growth, and the significance of the digital divide in the region, ASEAN leaders have been putting in place ICT strategies and initiatives at regional, country, and industry levels. The e-ASEAN Framework Agreement aims to promote ICT growth among and within ASEAN countries in the business, social, and government sectors by complementing national ICT development to set an environment conducive for competitive global integration.

Five task groups are identified to lead the private-public sector advisory for development in information infrastructure: e-commerce, ICT marketplace, ICT capacity, e-society, and e-government. The roles of the task groups were eventually subsumed into the e-ASEAN Business Council or e-ABC which has been proactively engaging CEO-level representatives from the private sectors to provide feedback on policy and regulatory issues, emerging technologies, industry and technology standards, cross-border issues, and removal of impediments.

The ICT-ization of ASEAN began as early as 1992. The countries have made significant growth notwithstanding the disruption of the Asian financial crisis and are mainly propelled by government commitment, private sector push, falling IT costs globally, and an increasing ICT resource pool. Independently the ASEAN countries embarked on nationwide ICT projects, legislations, incentives, investments, and research. These initiatives are geared toward building the ICT infrastructure, increasing awareness, upgrading skills, creating employment, attracting investments, technology and knowledge transfer, and diffusing ICT to public and private organizations, schools and homes.

Overall, the positive trend has paved the way for modernization in the less developed countries and greater innovation in the more developed ones. In some cases, technology makes it possible for latecomers to leapfrog certain developments and they may be in better position to align with current trends and future developments. For example, Cambodia is the first country in the world where mobile phone subscribers exceed the number of fixed-line subscribers. This also means that it does not have to go through the hassle and costs of upgrading old telephone networks if it had progressed in the typical manner of starting with providing the whole country with fixed analog lines.

e-ASEAN is catalytic in its role in ICT development in ASEAN. Though some of the pilot projects did not completely get off the ground, they were instrumental in providing the ideas, concepts, and experience for implementation of other projects and for defining the preliminary frameworks for the individual countries to execute their ICT strategies and plans. Today, all ASEAN countries have in place digital technology blueprints using the government sector to spearhead investments and applications of ICT in public services, activities, and programs. In addition, national capital expenditure is being allocated for expansion and upgrades of internal and external communications links (see Table 1.2).

Table 1.2   National ICT snapshots

Brunei	• Broadband network RAGAM21 which includes fiber optic cables to international gateway connectivity through submarine to Malaysia, Singapore, the Philippines, and the US. RAGAM21 provides the backbone and platform for e-commerce, e-government, distance learning, smart schools, and telemedicine. • B$1 billion allocation for e-government projects.
Cambodia	• NiDA (National Information Development Authority) to computerize government departments, remove "rural" barriers from the IT development, and work closely with donor countries, government agencies, industries, and community.
Indonesia	• SISFONAS 2010 (Sistem Informasi Nasional) national ICT blueprint concept framework to speed up e-government, promote ICT for all mainstream activities, connect to low tele-density areas, and proliferate broadband and wireless access.
Laos	• Masterplan (2003–2015) to implement basic infrastructure and ICT development. • LANIC (Lao National Internet Committee) to modernize public sector and provide IT access to private sector business
Malaysia	• Multimedia Super Corridor (MSC) aims to attract global and local ICT companies to undertake R&D on multi-media and communications products, solutions, and services and use MSC as a high-tech production base, global test bed, and regional operations hub for Asia.
Myanmar	• ICT Masterplan to stimulate ICT development, by attracting local and international partners to form a cluster of ICT-related business, supported by world-class infrastructure and technologies. • Myanmar ICT Development Corporation, a consortium of (50) local companies with the full support from the government-developed MICT Park project to create Myanmar ICT hub.

Table 1.2—continued

Philippines	• IT21 sets the vision and framework.
	• ICT development driven mainly by private sector telecommunication giants (PLDT, Globe) and ICT consortiums (TelicPhil).
Thailand	• National ICT Masterplan (2002–2006) promotes the ICT development and allocates over 135 billion baht in ICT development.
	• IT 2010 supersedes IT 2000 and commits to 60 million baht in e-government projects.
Singapore	• SingaporeOne islandwide broadband network for interactive multimedia applications and services.
	• Infocomm21 to develop new sources of growth, including arts and design.
	• S$620 million for additional e-government projects in 2006.
	• iN2015 masterplan for Next Generation networks including wireless broadband.
Vietnam	• ICT Masterplan to establish nationwide infocomm network, develop ICT skills, and implement IT to private and public sectors.

ICT Impact on Economy

The technological push and pull factors working in continuous tandem create a wheel of growth moving the economy forward. The countries with the highest infostate are the same countries with the highest GDP; likewise the same applies to the lowest infostate countries with the lowest GDP. That digital technology is strongly and directly related to economic growth makes ICT development one of the top priorities for national development.

This is not to say that only the ICT sector prospers and drives the world's economies. ICT and ICT-related suppliers will continue to play important roles in providing technologies and solutions to enhance business and social environments. But technology is facing a future of being commoditized as products become mainstream standard consumer items with declining hardware and packaged software prices. IBM has taken a bet on this in its sale of the still profitable PC business to China's Lenovo in order to focus on its enterprise solution and professional services businesses. The growth trend in ICT is anticipated in the provision of solutions and services to knowledge-based, technology-dependent sectors such as banking, finance, insurance, healthcare, real estate, tourism, aerospace, on-demand manufacturing, logistics, shipping, public services, education, security, and defense. According to the Organization for Economic Cooperation and Development (OECD), renowned ICT-producing countries like Germany and Japan have not had the kind of growth recorded in the US or Australia that are big technology users. The greater impact of ICT on the economy is therefore in the utilization of technology to raise efficiency and productivity in core industries while encouraging innovative products and services in existing and new markets.

Digitization is the initial process that brings forth transformation in our political, economic, and social environments. The formation of the e-ASEAN framework is a step forward for the region to implement digital networks, produce hardware and software, and apply knowledge-based systems.

US Defense Secretary Rumsfeld once stated, "If you look at a picture from the sky of the Korean Peninsula at night, South Korea is filled with lights and energy and vitality and a booming economy; North Korea is dark." There is more to that statement than the simple observation of light. The same was experienced when a visitor to Hong Kong's northern territories in the 1980s at night saw only darkness across the border on the China side. From the same spot, a very different picture is seen today. Chinese cities are mushrooming all over the country and building beyond their own capacity as economic growth escalates. The access to electricity, providing light to see in the dark and power to work machines, has been an important indicator of progress and prosperity from the start of the Industrial Revolution.

The impact of ICT on the economy in today's digital world is comparable to the bright and dark sides of the industrialized world. The enlightened economy is one that has access to quality information and communications, is able to make calculated decisions, has a clear analysis of current environments in order to project future markets, and enjoys better work and living conditions. Economies that do not have sufficient information and adequate communication channels are unable to acquire the relevant knowledge or connect to resources that could facilitate technology or knowledge transfer. Such economies will be exposed to low productivity and poor quality of goods and services, have no competitive advantage compared to the rest of the world, and eventually end up marginalized and left behind. Digital technology is to the knowledge-based 21st century what electricity was to the industrialized age.

chapter 2

Impact of Globalization on ASEAN

Southeast Asia ... must never remain static for anything static is as good as dead.[1]

Dato Sri Mohd Najib Tun Razak

Does the flap of a butterfly's wings in Brazil set off a tornado in Texas? This rhetorical and provocative question was first broached by Edward N. Lorenz, an American mathematician and meteorologist in 1972. The *Butterfly Effect*, a phrase that spun out of Lorenz's chaos theory, is most commonly linked to the long-term and major effects of a dynamic system as a result of initial insignificant changes. To illustrate this, we recall the May 2000 incident when a 23-year-old Filipino fiddling with computer codes inadvertently released his *ILOVEYOU* script on the Internet. The virus which attached itself to every contact in a computer's address book was first discovered in Hong Kong and incessantly caused widespread email outages around the world within hours. Economic damage was estimated to be US$10 billion, making "love bug" the most damaging computer worm ever. Such is the effect of a single seemingly trivial act in a dynamic environment.

In today's interconnected, interdependent world, this effect is associated with the speed and impact of an event, an action, or a decision in a global system where more countries and organizations are exposed to external physical and networked environments. Globalization has been defined in many ways and referred to as various terms—process, integration, transformation, intensification, exchange, movement, development. However, the most undeniable, concrete

---

[1] Dato Sri Mohd Najib Tun Razak, speech given at the ASEAN 100 Leadership Forum, Singapore, September 29, 2005.

factor of globalization is that it brings about continuous pervasive, prevalent, and often unprecedented changes. The obvious changes are in technological advances, political policies, legal frameworks, and economic development. These in turn influence market orientations and business outlooks. On the other hand, socio-cultural changes are less apparent, harder to determine, and more complex to predict. In today's context, socio-cultural changes are not confined within geographical territories but are brought about by transnational networked communities.

This form of change is often outside the normal environment scan as the data is not easily collated and the noticeable component may appear too insignificant initially for organizations to be bothered with until the change becomes too large to ignore. Traditional systems based and planned on linear processes, projections, trends, known rules, and controlled growth will not be able to respond effectively to changes, and therefore will be disadvantaged and marginalized. For example, *open-source* can be defined as a transnational "techno" socio-culture of the 21st century. Linux, an open-source PC-based UNIX operating system, was developed by an informal group of computer enthusiasts in their free time. It was made available freely with a copyright license that allows modifications to be made by anyone and distributed to anyone. Linux users all over the world loyally support the software with near-religious devotion and make all efforts to improve its functionalities and fix all problems, making it a mainstream computer standard (competing directly with Microsoft Windows).

Another lesson learned from globalization is the change in international trade and the nature of imports and exports. Traditionally, a country imports raw materials and manufactures finished products for the local and overseas markets. Countries with raw materials export them and import finished foreign products. Globalization in recent years has allowed the flow of goods, services, capital, and labor almost seamlessly between countries and across time zones. End-producers are no longer only the developed countries because competitive pressures have forced them to manufacture their goods and service their products where labor is much cheaper. For example, an American brand designed in Europe, made in China, and serviced by a call center in India is a commonly accepted fact today.

It is therefore conceivable that any place on earth even without technical know-how can be turned into a manufacturing hub and any country with open-market policies can be an end-producer in the global market. This is possible because technology can be easily transferred, people adequately trained, raw materials imported or produced, and infrastructures built. This is what global integration is about. Countries must react positively to the changes and regions must accept integration as a way toward progress and prosperity. The speed of acceptance of this change will determine the rate of development, and thus the growth of a country or a region.

This is of course easier said than done. Different countries are made up of different demographics, cultures, laws, geographies, and stages of development. Cosmopolitan lifestyles are found only in the big cities but that is not the only indication of globalization. Absolute poverty exists even in the richest countries and the gap between the affluent and the impoverished is not improving. Some have blamed globalization as the cause of increasing poverty but that is an inconclusive accusation. However, this does not mean that globalization is the all-encompassing solution to the world's problems either. Globalization has its risks too. The Asian crisis in 1997 attests to the negative outcome of a country's financial liberalization to global markets. But the same economies hurt by the crisis were the early beneficiaries of globalization that had enjoyed three decades of strong growth compared to their closed-economy neighbors.

Change, whether incremental or radical, is the shift from the known to the unknown, and from the old to the new. Globalization is about changes from homogeneous societies and closed economies to cross-cultures and free markets. It induces proliferation of technology and knowledge, promotes capitalism and wealth accumulation, and in general improves living standards. However, changes brought about by globalization do not always produce desirable results. Some of the problems faced are the spread of infectious diseases, propagation of extremist ideologies, children-related abuse, rampant counterfeiting leading to health problems and life-threatening situations, and environment degradation.

Understanding the changes and the impact of changes is important in strategic thinking and management today. Globalization has evolved from an embryonic form of commerce system to a dynamic set of complex political, financial, and legal structures that defines and supports the way countries with dissimilar languages and customs integrate into a global economy. Organizations that analyze their strengths, weaknesses, opportunities, and threats (SWOT) before defining their strategies will miss the most crucial factor in the formulation: change, the infinite variable. Open economies are especially susceptible to changes. Organizations engaged in global markets must apply an "outside-in" approach by analyzing the threats, opportunities, weaknesses, strengths (TOWS) in order to produce a more relevant strategy for future business landscape. Globalization has accelerated change and this has major impact on cost structures, demand and supply mechanics, and the relationships between producer and consumer.

Globalization Change Agents

The first era of globalization (let us call it Globalization 1.0) began in the 1400s about the time when Zheng He set sail in the east and Christopher Columbus in the west, both in search of new lands, raw materials, and trading opportunities for their respective monarchs. At that time, sovereign decree presided over all matters and affairs under their rule. Power was in the hands of those who had control of people (muscle power), beasts of burden (horse power), and nature (agriculture and wind power). These resources were the fundamental forces of change in the exploration of new frontiers, accumulation of wealth, and show of physical might and control.

The second era (Globalization 2.0) came about in the 1800s with the practical and widespread use of the steam engine leading to mechanization and urbanization where raw material could be harnessed more efficiently, goods produced more easily, and masses of people could travel faster and further. It was the golden age of industrialization when massive railway networks and the first factories were built. Territorial explorations transformed into colonization; commerce moved from the state to individually owned businesses or private organizations; and power shifted as a new world order was defined from those who had resources to those who knew how to make use of these resources.

Some have argued that the third era or Globalization 3.0 started after World War II in the mid-1940s when computers made their debut and trade resumed with the formation of transnational organizations such as the United Nations. Others contend that Globalization 3.0 began at the end of the Cold War and the introduction of the Internet in the early 1990s. Regardless of the definition, we infer that the recent period of globalization is driven fundamentally by technology and politically through world peace. Table 2.1 summarizes all these globalization events.

As we are writing this book, a new effect of globalization is happening with growing 'momentum as well as growing anxiety. The "Wimbledon Effect," concerning the infiltration of foreign ownerships of national companies, is sweeping across the world. This situation draws comparison to the 129-year-old English Wimbledon tennis championship that has been won by non-English players since 1936. The attempt by China National Offshore Oil Corporation (CNOOC) to buy Unocal, a US oil company, was obstructed by US lawmakers and eventually Unocal merged with Chevron, another US corporation instead. When British shipping and logistics giant P&O was sold to Dubai Ports World, Americans protested against the running of their ports by a company based in the Arab Middle East, fearful that national security would be undermined. Submitting to pressure, the American ports remained in US control. The takeover by Singapore's Temasek Holdings of Thailand's Shin Corp, a family-owned telecommunications conglomerate of former Thai Prime Minister Thaksin Shinawatra, brought thousands of Thais to the streets to protest against the billions of dollars of tax-free profits

Table 2.1   History of globalization

Era	Period	Dynamic force of change	Key agents of change	Challenge
Globalization 1.0	1492–1800	Muscle power, horse power, wind power, steam power	Countries	
Globalization 2.0	1800–2000	Hardware— from steamships and railroads in the beginning to telephones and mainframe computers toward the end	Multinational companies	• Where does my company fit into the global economy? • How does it take advantage of the opportunities? • How can I go global and collaborate with others through my company?
Globalization 3.0	2000–	Software—all sorts of new applications— in conjunction with the creation of a global fiber-optic network	Individuals	• Where do I fit into the global competition and opportunities of the day? • How can I, on my own, collaborate with others globally?

made from the deal by the prime minister's relatives. The public outcry snowballed into weekly protests.

In the last 600 years, the rate of globalization has increased exponentially. In 1865 Reuters news agency was the first in Europe to report the assassination of US President Abraham Lincoln 12 days after the event. The news created shock waves across the continent.

Today news from any part of the world is broadcast worldwide instantaneously in various mediums and on various devices—TV, radio, the Internet, and wireless communications.

Mass media communication, such as the Internet, offers easy access to information, transforming the average man-in-the-street into a knowledge-based world citizen. Empowerment of the masses creates a need for transparency and the call for more transparency in all organizations. This empowerment is not necessarily troublesome for a country but makes a fundamental mindset change necessary. For a country to be successful at positioning itself globally and enjoying the benefits of open-market conditions, the mindset change must come from the top.

Political and Legal Changes

Globalization at political levels is crucial in effecting major and immediate long-term changes to an economy. The two big stars of globalization—China and India—have extremely different political systems, China being politically the world's largest communist country and India the world's largest liberal democracy. Both countries had experienced widespread poverty, inefficiencies, and poor living standards before they adopted open-market policies and instituted economic reforms.

China's political change and reforms started in the late 1970s when party leader Deng Xiao Ping's "open-door policy" promoted a shift from its Soviet-style centrally planned economy to a more market-oriented economy by relaxing price controls, focusing on foreign trade and investment, reorganizing state-owned enterprises and agricultural sectors, increasing productivity, and opening its previously closed markets to competition. The result has been a six-fold increase of GDP since 1978 with average annual GDP rate above 9% for the past 28 years. China joined the World Trade Organization (WTO) in 2001 and at the end of 2005, it became the fourth largest economy in the world with a GDP of approximately US$2.25 trillion, and the second largest in the world after the US by purchasing power parity (PPP) at US$8,158 trillion.

India, like Myanmar, Malaysia, and Singapore, was under British rule until the end of World War II. Since independence, the government has exercised strict control over private sector participation, foreign trade and foreign direct investment. India has been maintaining cordial relationships with many nations and has been a long-time supporter of the United Nations. The turning point in India's politics came when Rajiv Gandhi became Prime Minister in 1984. He began to dismantle the elaborate red-tape system of government quotas, tariffs, and permits, and started to modernize the telecommunications industry, improve the education system, expand science and technology initiatives, and forge closer links with the US. Indian software companies profited from the Y2K scare which created worldwide demand for battalions of computer programmers. Amidst political battles and intermittent unrests, the economy grew to become the fourth largest in the world as measured by PPP at US$3.36 trillion and the tenth largest in the world with GDP of approximately US$691.87 billion. India was the second fastest growing major economy in the world (after China), with a GDP growth rate of 8.1% at the end of the first quarter of 2005–2006.

Politicians, policy makers, and business leaders must work together to make globalization beneficial for all. Political and legal changes toward open-market economies pave the way for opportunities by removing restrictions and liberalizing the flow of capital, people, and goods. But liberalization is only effective when done in tandem with credible control mechanisms. The challenge is balancing the positive and negative effects of globalization, and providing for responsible regulatory measures to ensure that a country does not suffer adversely as a result of over- or under-exposure to globalization.

The Asian crisis was a test of a country's, and to a certain extent, a region's resilience and reaction to external changes caused by globalization. Thailand, the first falling pin in the crisis, accepted the rescue package from the International Monetary Fund (IMF), floated its currency, and saw its economy contract by 10.5% before recovering two years later. The Philippines raised overnight interest rates from

15% to 24% to defend the peso but the currency fell over 50% and the country went into a recession for three years. Malaysia in the line of attack saw its currency spiral down, forcing its central bank to revert to a fixed exchange rate system for its ringgit. Indonesia had a sizeable trade surplus and foreign reserve before the crisis but crumbled as the rupiah was abandoned for safer currencies even after the IMF stepped in with a US$23 billion rescue package.

The three "Asian Tigers"—Hong Kong, South Korea, and Singapore—were not spared from the crisis. Barely three months after Hong Kong was handed over to China, its monetary authority spent more than US$1 billion to defend the Hong Kong dollar against speculators and poured approximately US$15 billion into the stock market. One of the world's largest economies, South Korea had to be bailed out by IMF and took the bitter pill of harsh economic reforms to regain its global position. Singapore, being a small and open economy, was indirectly affected by the crisis and embarked on a series of internal policies and reforms to strengthen its competitiveness.

In 2003, globalization showed its ugly side again when SARS cast a deadly gloom in Asia and other parts of the world. The opening of new markets had resulted in the rapid spread of offshore facilities, products and services, people, and unfortunately, diseases as well. At the height of the SARS epidemic, the worst-hit economies came to a standstill as all transport and human-related activities were stopped, reduced, or delayed. The recent warnings by the World Health Organization (WHO) of a possible avian flu pandemic take into account the increase in global mobility and the painful experiences from SARS.

The years following the Asian crisis and SARS bore witness to renewed marginalization arising from uneven and unequal growth as the world continues to globalize while developing countries struggle to rebuild and reform their economies. Countries and groups that felt marginalized are unhappy with the framework for globalization and criticized that it was designed by the rich countries for the rich countries.

Economic Changes

Before the dot-com bubble burst, many newly listed companies with
initial public offer (IPO) money were feverishly acquiring other
companies without fully calculating the true cost of integration
and management of the combined entities. To most, mergers and
acquisitions (M&As) were a quick way for companies to gain access to
technologies, customers, and markets. Besides the obvious benefits of
expansion and diversification, M&As serve to strengthen a company's
position especially in the global markets through economies of scale
and international branding. An M&A is fundamentally a corporate
finance tool to boost shareholder value by increasing assets or tax
write-offs. In the past 25 years, there have been two major M&A
waves, one in the late 1980s and the other after the 1997 financial
crisis. Expanding global economies gave rise to a surge in global
finance, and a new trend of cross-border M&A emerged in recent
years. These cross-border M&As were the key drivers of foreign
direct investment (FDI) in the last decade.

FDI is a growth-enhancing supplement and attracting FDI has
been a key part of national development strategies for many countries.
For years, economic development, trade liberalization, and FDI have
been closely related. Besides M&As, FDI comes in the form of joint
ventures (JV), alliances and *greenfield* investments.[2] According to data
released in early January 2006 by the UN Conference on Trade and
Development (UNCTAD), worldwide FDI soared to an estimated
US$897 billion in 2005—up 29% from a year ago. Determinants
of FDI are:

- Market size and prospects
- Projected growth
- Physical infrastructure such as utilities and telecommunications
- Financial framework
- Legal and regulatory structure

---

[2] Greenfield investment is direct investment in new facilities or the expansion of existing
facilities.

- Economic incentives, such as free trade agreements
- Political stability
- Labor cost, productivity, and innovation
- Investment environment, such as tax concessions, grants, and subsidies
- Natural resources

Progressively liberalizing trade and FDI encourage market-driven regionalization in high-performing economies. When one takes into account the accelerating effects of the Triple C theory proposed by Lim Chong Yah in his Trinity Growth theory, the impact is not just quite astounding, but resounding too. The Triple C Theory postulates that a modern economy is propelled by three engines: (1) the domestic engine, (2) the regional engine, and (3) the global engine. The three growth engines are linked to one another through economic connectivity of which geographical neighborliness may be an important factor.[3]

In the last 25 years, Japan provided much of the FDI in the emerging ASEAN countries for the manufacturing and electronics industries. Concentration of economic activities led to economic integration among these countries. Production shifted from local firms to networks of regional production to institution-led regionalization. The forces behind market-driven and institutionally driven regionalization are rapid economic growth, FDI liberalization, free trade agreements, regional integration, and globalization.

Globalization or Regionalization

Following the failed WTO ministerial conference, economist Alan Rugman wrote *The End of Globalization*.[4] In his radical analysis of the role of international trade bodies, non-governmental organizations, and multinational enterprises, the author argued that globalization of business is in fact a myth and a homogeneous marketplace is merely

---

[3] Lim Chong Yah, "China in the World Economy," *Nanyang Business Review*, Vol. 4, No. 1, pp. 5–14, 2005.

[4] Alan Rugman, *The End of Globalization*. Random House Business Books, 2000.

a fiction. In his view, international economic activity has been driven by just 500 multinational enterprises operating in the triad of North America, the European Union, and Japan (and updated recently to Asia). These corporations are neither globally monolithic nor politically powerful but produce and distribute goods for highly competitive regional markets (for example, 90% of cars produced in Europe are sold in Europe).

Rugman classified international companies as home-region oriented if they have at least 50% of sales in their home region; bi-region if over 20% of sales are in two regions in the triad; host-region if over 50% of sales is in a triad region other than home; and global if sales in each triad region are between 20 and 50%. From his research on 365 of the world's largest multinational corporations, he found that only nine are global, 11 are host-oriented, 25 are bi-regional, and the remaining 320 are home-region oriented. The observation is that most multinational companies in the world are only strong in their home region and one other region at the most. This study draws the conclusion that regionalization is more important in driving economic growth than globalization.

Regionalization is being brought about by globalization through a series of interdependent, overlapping, consecutive, challenging, and reactive events. The European Union (EU) model is testament to the success and importance of regionalization in a globalized marketplace. The region reduces anomalies in regulations between different countries by having a common single market; a customs union; a single currency, the Euro, managed by a single central bank; common agricultural, trade, and fisheries policies; and foreign and security policies where EU citizens can move freely within internal borders, thus creating a single space of mobility to live, travel, work, and invest.

Closer home, the need to regionalize is even more pronounced. The Asian miracle in the 1980s led to a call for more effective economic cooperation across the Asia-Pacific region and ultimately the formation of the Asia-Pacific Economic Cooperation (APEC) comprising a group of 21 Pacific Rim countries, including the US. China, India, Indonesia, Pakistan, Bangladesh, and Japan are amongst the most populated countries in the world. This helps to make Asia a formidable size in terms of labor supply and consumer market. With open-market policies, globalization will increase the competitiveness of this region, turning it into the 21st century growth locus.

As a regional trade bloc, ASEAN has begun several initiatives to promote free trade and economic growth within the region and with global trading partners. Some of these initiatives were not completely followed through due to implementation weaknesses and global changes. On the whole, the spirit of ASEAN captured in the original declaration remains to represent the collective will of its member nations for peace and prosperity for its people. At the social and humanitarian front, this has been demonstrated in its cohesiveness to combat terrorism and the unprompted aid given to the victims of the tsunami disaster in December 2004.

Efforts to boost economic cooperation and regional integration are formulated in the ASEAN Free Trade Area (AFTA) agreement which covers trade, investment, industry, services, finance, agriculture, forestry, energy, transportation and communication, intellectual property, small and medium enterprises, and tourism. The primary goals of AFTA are to increase ASEAN's competitive edge as a production base in the world market through the elimination within ASEAN, of tariffs and non-tariff barriers and to attract more foreign direct investments to ASEAN. The establishment of AFTA represents a level of economic harmony among the member nations with politically diverse doctrines such as the Philippines which follows a democratic system and Vietnam with a communist system.

From the world's viewpoint, ASEAN can also be seen as a buffer zone between China and India, and between China and Japan. Multinational corporations who have long established production facilities in ASEAN countries have moved their plants and service centers to lower-cost China and India but continued with their bases in the Southeast Asian countries where they have had a longer presence and commitment. Japan is keen to create a huge Asian free trade bloc of 16 nations to integrate economies in the region to rival the EU and the North American Free Trade Agreement (NAFTA) which includes the US, Canada, and Mexico. The Asian free trade bloc aims to include China, India, Australia, New Zealand, South Korea, and ASEAN. The enthusiasm for Japan to spearhead this was partly due to the difficult relations she is having with China because of historical reasons and when attempts by Japan to accelerate a regional free trade agreement with China were stalled. On the other hand, China already has a free trade agreement with ASEAN (ACFTA). In May 2006 ASEAN signed a Trade-in-Goods (TIG) agreement with South Korea under the Framework Agreement on Comprehensive Economic Cooperation. The free trade agreement between India and ASEAN is planned for implementation in 2007, making ASEAN the inaugural gateway to access the world's fast-growing economies.

Challenges for ASEAN

As the turn-of-the-millennium clouds of gloom precipitated, the ASEAN countries are again aligning themselves for economic growth in this region. Regionalization and open-market policies have enhanced cross-border relationships and accelerated trade for ASEAN countries. The admission of Vietnam, Cambodia, Laos, and Myanmar will create new markets as well as competition for low-cost production and services. However, the more developed ASEAN countries have the advantage of better infrastructure, processes, technological know-how, and well-trained people and are therefore best positioned to add value to their neighbors. In essence, all ASEAN countries will progress in a concerted manner when cooperating as one single bloc.

The region is now heading for an upturn but the biggest challenge is growth sustainability for both the established and new ASEAN members. In the book *Repositioning Asia: From Bubble to Sustainable Economy*, authors Philip Kotler and Hermawan Kartajaya use the Sustainable Model to explain how small and medium-sized enterprises (SMEs) can build sustainability to survive in the ever-changing landscape. We refer to this model again here (as it can be applied to ASEAN as a comparable global SME), to discuss the different phases the region has gone through and the challenges ahead. Our Sustainable Model is a re-representation of trade cycles looped into a

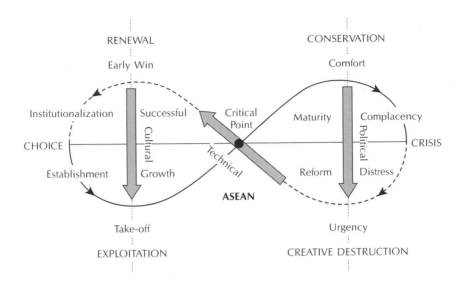

Figure 2.1   ASEAN's sustainability at critical point

horizontal "8" and the turn of cycles associated with the various stages of development (see Figure 2.1).

Except for Thailand, the four founding ASEAN countries gained their independence after World War II and the complete decolonization marked the beginning of self-governing for the first time after years of foreign rule. The 1950s and 60s hosted the arrival of baby-boomers and the rise of the US as a superpower. This was the period when ASEAN was being established and its members were attracting FDI from the US, Europe, and Japan. ASEAN was taking off in an unprecedented course, inviting multinational companies to set up factories and businesses in this low-cost, resource-rich region. Economic expansion in the capitalized world caused demand for goods and services to exceed supply. ASEAN began to prosper as a trading hub, a production base, and an exporter of raw materials.

Growth continued astoundingly albeit marked by sporadic cyclical downturns and domestic squabbles. Standards of living improved as ASEAN continued to serve the flood of international companies bringing their businesses offshore. The region was becoming affluent, comfortable, and complacent. Flushed with capital and queues of investment bankers waiting to be received, ASEAN was tempted to borrow excessively. Trade imbalance and short-term debt ballooned. Investors' belief of a once economic miracle was removed which inevitably led to the 1997 financial crisis. After the crisis, ASEAN leaders put in place corrective policies and painful measures to re-establish confidence and to ensure stability to turn the economies around. Most of the countries have already posted positive growth but ASEAN is at a critical point now.

There are many challenges awaiting the region that may impede continuous growth. Some of these can be predicted and prepared for, others are unforeseeable and need to be dealt with in the best possible manner. Individual countries must put in place a set of insurance plans to safeguard their economies from being left out of global developments. Some of the factors that will determine continuous growth in ASEAN are

- Preventive measures to maintain its economies in the event of pandemics, terrorist attacks, political breakouts, or natural disasters.
- Contingency plans to prepare for globalization backlash if developed countries turned protectionist in order to keep their labor unions and voters happy.
- Resources and assistance given to local companies to grow regionally and be integrated into the global markets.
- Investment in technology, infrastructure, people development, and environment management.
- Good governance practices in private and public sectors.
- Reserves to support its economies in times of world economic downturn or high energy prices.

Heads of states must stay committed to the ASEAN cause and strive for the common good of the region. Business leaders must promote regional (not just national) achievements and carve the ASEAN brand globally. Overall, ASEAN must build the stamina, credibility, and enthusiasm to renew itself successfully in all aspects—financial, legal, economics, technology, politics, environment, social, and cultural. In addition, ASEAN must stay relevant to the world, be able to react rationally to changes, and have the leadership to steer the region forward. Understanding the challenges and realizing the opportunities are crucial in formulating the right strategies and execution plans to perform well in the ever-changing global landscape.

In the next chapter, we will discuss more about ASEAN as an organization, as a community, and as a region; how the region will fare in the 21st century as the world evolves; how it may change from within; and how it would react to external volatility.

chapter 3

The Future Market of ASEAN

ASEAN is moving gradually but progressively towards a shared future.[1]

Lee Hsien Loong

Scientists have attributed the reasons for geese flying in a "V" formation to flight and visual optimization. The lead bird breaks the air and stirs updrafts at the other birds' wing tips. In the updrafts, the birds behind can get more distance with less energy. Each bird flies slightly above the bird in front of him, resulting in good visibility and reduction of wind resistance. In this way, the geese can fly for a long time before they must stop for rest. Birds take turns to lead because of fatigue but all geese stay in the "V" shape to avoid misalignments and increased workload.

The flying geese formation is an excellent demonstration of the social and economic advantages of group cooperation and dynamics. The "Asian miracle" has often been compared to the flying geese formation to explain the pattern of economic development and industry lifecycles, the rise and fall of specific industries or countries, and the shift of industries from one country to another. First discussed publicly in 1961 by Japanese scholar Kaname Akamatsu, it explains the shifting of industries from Japan to newly industrialized economies (NIE) and further to ASEAN, China, and India. It also shows that Japan, being the "lead goose" for over 30 years, had slipped into stagnation in the last ten years while China and India took over as the growth engines in Asia as the two emerging economies aligned themselves to take the most advantage of globalization.

---

[1] Lee Hsien Loong, speech given at the ASEAN 100 Leadership Forum, Singapore, September 28, 2005.

ASEAN-5, referring to the five founding members of Indonesia, Malaysia, the Philippines, Singapore, and Thailand, was very much part of the Asian miracle and flying geese formation. The group enjoyed years of phenomenal growth but has also experienced an era of hardship as a result of globalization. Since recovering from the Asian financial crisis, ASEAN has achieved a higher level of maturity and is more rooted to its common goals for peace, progress, and prosperity. With the changing global business landscape, ASEAN-5 and the newer members of Brunei, Vietnam, Laos, Cambodia, and Myanmar must commit to integration and alignment to achieve the most favorable position with their collective strengths and comparative advantages in the light of fresh and aggressive world competition.

In this chapter, we will discuss ASEAN as an organization, as a community, and as a region and how it is changing from within in its proactive efforts to integrate globally and be properly prepared to react to the external volatility of the 21st century. We will also highlight the challenges and opportunities faced by expanding companies in ASEAN as markets get bigger but at the same time more complex.

ASEAN—An Organization, a Community, and a Region

ASEAN stands for the Association of Southeast Asian Nations and was established in 1967 in Bangkok by the five original members of Indonesia, Malaysia, the Philippines, Singapore, and Thailand. These members initially represented a solidarity body to promote peace and stability in the light of communist expansion at that time and to control insurgency within their own borders. After the Vietnam War the organization embarked on a program of economic cooperation, which floundered in the mid-1980s, only to be revived in the early 1990s by a Thai proposal for a regional "free trade area." In 1984, Brunei joined ASEAN, followed by Vietnam in 1995, Laos and Myanmar in 1997, and Cambodia in 1999.

The highest decision-making body is the annual ASEAN Summit meeting held by the ASEAN heads of state and government (see Figure 3.1). In general, ASEAN makes decisions based on member consensus and consultations with 11 dialog partners, namely Australia,

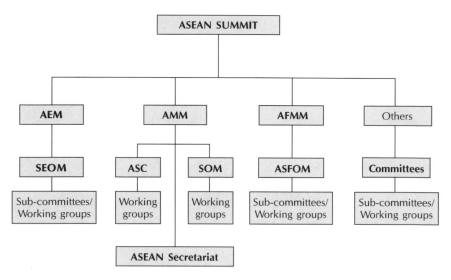

AEM: ASEAN Economic Ministers
AMM: ASEAN Ministerial Meeting
AFMM: ASEAN Finance Ministers Meeting
SEOM: Senior Economic Officials Meeting
ASC: ASEAN Standing Committee
SOM: Senior Officials Meeting
ASFOM: ASEAN Senior Finance Officials Meeting

Figure 3.1   Illustrative ASEAN organizationl structure

Canada, China, European Union, India, Japan, New Zealand, South Korea, Russia, the US, and the United Nations Development Program (UNDP). Decisions made at the Summit are executed at the ministerial levels and supported by senior officials and working groups.

Security has always been a sensitive but essential agenda item. Major ASEAN accords are made with a strong flavor for peace and harmony with one another and with the world at large. In 1994, the ASEAN Regional Forum or ARF was established to promote external dialogs in political and security matters as a means of building cooperative ties with states in the Asia-Pacific region. The participants in ARF include the ten ASEAN members and Australia, Canada, China, European Union, India, Japan, North and South Korea, Myanmar, Mongolia, New Zealand, Pakistan, Papua New Guinea, Russia, and the

US. ASEAN Vision 2020, a commitment made in 1997 by ASEAN Heads of States, aims to build a zone of peace, dynamic development, caring community, and outward-looking ASEAN by the year 2020. In 2006, ASEAN agreed in principle to speed up efforts to create a single market by 2015. The agreement came at the start of an annual conference of the region's economic ministers, who will focus on achieving closer integration in response to competition from China and India.

Since ASEAN was formed 39 years ago, there have been no major political or social conflicts among its member nations and the region has achieved its goal for peace and harmony. Economic development surged and economic cooperation grew in importance. ASEAN member countries have progressively lowered their intra-regional tariffs through the Common Effective Preferential Tariff (CEPT) Scheme for the ASEAN Free Trade Area (AFTA). The strategic objective of AFTA is to increase the region's competitive advantage as a single production unit by eliminating tariff and non-tariff barriers among the member countries to promote greater efficiency and productivity. To encourage the flows of investment, technologies, and skills in the region, the ASEAN Investment Area (AIA) and ASEAN Industrial Cooperation Scheme (AICO) were established. AIA is designed to bind member countries to eliminate obstacles to investment, liberalize investment rules and policies, and open up industries to foreign investment. AICO aims to promote joint manufacturing industrial activities between ASEAN-based companies.

Inter-governmental bodies cooperate with each other for education, agriculture, food, tourism, environment, and life sciences; and with organizations such as ASEAN Chambers of Commerce and Industry, ASEAN Business Forum, ASEAN Tourism Association, ASEAN Council on Petroleum, ASEAN Ports Association, ASEAN Vegetable Oils Club, ASEAN Institutes for Strategic and International Studies, and the Regional Haze Action Plan. In addition, regional integration is being pursued for trans-ASEAN projects such as land, sea, and air transportation networks; interoperability and interconnectivity of telecommunications; and energy networks, power grids, and gas pipelines.

An outward-looking ASEAN pays to be involved in international affairs and active participation in groups such as Asia-Pacific Economic Cooperation (APEC), the Asia-Europe Meeting (ASEM), and the East Asia-Latin America Forum (EALAF). Diplomatic missions have been made in major capital cities in Brussels, London, Paris, Washington D.C., Tokyo, Canberra, Ottawa, Wellington, Geneva, Seoul, New Delhi, New York, Beijing, Moscow, and Islamabad. For example, the European Union (EU) relations with ASEAN are based on the 1980 Cooperation Agreement. The EU represents ASEAN's third largest trading partner, providing its second largest export market after the US and just ahead of Japan. For the EU, ASEAN is its fourth largest trading partner, ahead of China. With its growing export-led economies and a developing domestic market of more than 540 million people, ASEAN is a region of increasing economic and strategic importance, whose current and longer-term potential continues to attract strong commercial interest from the EU industries.

Although the multifaceted ASEAN has accomplished a great deal, it is not without issues. ASEAN was criticized by international human rights communities for failing to act to resolve the conflict between Indonesia and East Timor. The acceptance of Myanmar into ASEAN drew considerable condemnation from the West and has been a thorny issue since. The ongoing sagas between Singapore and Malaysia over various issues; between Malaysia and Thailand over the restive southern Thai border; and among the Philippines, Malaysia, and Vietnam (and China) over the Spratly Islands are due to the non-interference and non-intervention policy adopted by ASEAN members that existing conflict prevention mechanisms can only address inter-state conflicts. Often pressured to do more by external groups, there is no clear right or wrong about handling the issues. This is the way the ASEAN policy works to keep the individual countries independent in handling their own domestic affairs and bilateral relationships in alignment with the principles of the United Nations.

The challenge for ASEAN as an organization has always been to balance members' rights of sovereignty and to maintain its credibility as a progressive international organization committed to peace, economic growth, and a more egalitarian region. The ASEAN Declaration made in Bangkok on August 8, 1967 is fully endorsed by generations of state leaders of its member countries and stands firm to this day with continuous efforts to work together as a single community. It states that

> The Association represents the collective will of the nations to bind themselves together in friendship and cooperation and, through joint efforts and sacrifices, secure for their peoples and for posterity the blessings of peace, freedom, and prosperity.

The ASEAN Economic Community (AEC) is based on the three pillars of economic cooperation, political and security cooperation, and socio-cultural cooperation. It attempts to bring together capital, goods, services, and human resources into a single market and production base. This integration calls for the acceleration of free trade and business facilitation, upgrading of small and medium-sized companies, and enhancing the attractiveness of ASEAN as an investment destination.

For the region to enjoy sustained growth, it must maintain a safe and secure environment for its people and its investors. The ASEAN Security Community (ASC) was established to encourage sharing of norms; conflict prevention and resolution; and peace-building through positive political development (see Figure 3.2). ASC is the interactive force for ARF and ASEAN's dialog partners. ASC is used as a vehicle to combat terrorism and other transnational crimes such as illicit goods and human trafficking.

For many years history and the arts were shoved into the corridors of time while the countries strived for economic development and dealt with matters of survival for the people. With growing awareness and increasing interest in heritage and eco-tours, special care and preservation are now being given to nature reserves, breeding grounds for endangered species, ancient sites, and relics. The ASEAN Socio-Cultural Community (ASCC) was formed to represent the social and cultural interests of the ASEAN people as the region moves toward economic integration and globalization. Resources will be allocated for education, training, science and technology development, job

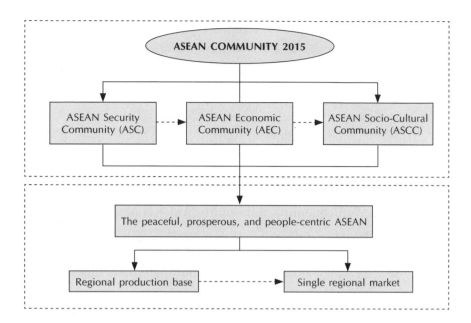

Figure 3.2   ASEAN Community 2015

creation, and social protection. ASCC will focus on functional systems that address poverty, equity, and health impact of economic growth; environmental control; natural resource management to meet current and future needs; and the preservation and promotion of the region's unique cultural heritage and identity.

ASEAN recognized that as much as the region is diverse in its cultures and customs, the ten member countries are also at different stages of economic development and readiness to integrate globally. There exists a disparity between the "traditional" economies and the knowledge-based "new" economies (see Table 3.1).

At the tenth ASEAN Summit in 2004 in Vientiane, Laos, the Vientiane Action Program (VAP) was unveiled as an instrument to unify and cross-link the strategies and goals of the AEC, ASC, and ASCC. VAP will also be an integral part of the action plans and programs building up to the realization of the goals of ASEAN Vision 2015. Through the implementation of VAP over a six-year period, ASEAN intends to narrow the development gap among member

Table 3.1 Disparity between the "traditional" economies and the knowledge-based "new" economies

	Traditional economies	New economies
Markets	Stable	Dynamic
Scope of competition	National (or regional)	Global
Organizational form	Hierarchical—bureaucratic	Networked—entrepreneurial
Key production factor	Labor and capital	Knowledge and innovation
Importance of research	Moderate	Critical
Nature of employment	Stable	Risk and opportunity
Regulation	Command and control	Market-oriented flexibility

Source: 2003 Report of the ASEAN Eminent Persons Group (EPG) on Vision 2020.

countries in order to speed up its integration into the global markets. Exotic, traditional Southeast Asia is fast transforming into "Business ASEAN" with vast opportunities for development and growth.

ASEAN Business Landscape

Economic growth rebounded after the financial crisis with GDP real growth rates increased for all ASEAN countries except Myanmar in 2004, and surpassing Japan and the UK. Trade grew from US$10 billion in 1967 when ASEAN was first formed to over US$1 trillion in 2005. Industrial production improved especially for the new members Cambodia and Vietnam (see Table 3.2).

Table 3.2   ASEAN 2004 statistics summary

Country	Population (thousands) Source: ASEAN Annual Report 2004–05	Land area (sq km) Source: ASEAN Annual Report 2004–05	GDP per capita (US$) Source: CIA	GDP: Real growth rate % Source: CIA	Industrial production growth rate % Source: CIA	Merchandise trade (US$ millions) Source: ASEAN Annual Report 2004–05	Foreign direct investment (US$ millions) Source: UNCTAD
Brunei	373	5,765	23,600	3.20	5.00	6,585	103
Cambodia	13,589	181,035	2,000	5.40	22.00	5,414	131
Indonesia	216,410	1,890,754	3,500	4.90	10.50	122,339	1,023
Laos	5,760	236,800	1,900	6.00	9.70	1,004	17
Malaysia	25,580	330,257	9,700	7.10	10.20	221,471	4,624
Myanmar	54,745	676,577	1,700	−1.30	na	5,034	556
Philippines	82,664	300,000	5,000	5.90	5.00	76,940	469
Singapore	4,240	697	27,800	8.10	11.10	363,431	16,060
Thailand	64,469	513,254	8,100	6.10	8.50	190,446	1,064
Vietnam	82,022	330,363	2,700	7.70	16.00	55,261	1,610
Total	549,852	4,465,502				1,047,925	25,657

Foreign direct investments (FDI) into ASEAN rose from US$17 billion in 2003 to US$26 billion in 2004. This was mainly due to the region's efforts to improve the investment environment after 1997 and the overall growth in Asia. Greenfield investments continue to be important in the manufacturing sector while the services sector is deemed to be a growth area with the gradual opening up of finance, telecommunications, transportation and logistics, and retail businesses. Cross-border merger and acquisition (M&A) cases increased from 168 in 2002 to 185 in 2003 as ASEAN rode on the global M&A wave. The increase was in areas of finance, manufacturing, telecommunications, and business services in Indonesia, Malaysia, Myanmar, the Philippines, and Vietnam. According to the United Nations Conference on Trade and Development (UNCTAD) World Investment Report 2005, Asia received US$148 billion in investments and was the top destination of FDI among developing countries (total of US$380 billion) in 2004. China and Hong Kong continue to draw the highest investments, accounting for two-thirds of all FDI in Asia. They in turn are responsible for 58% of the US$69 billion FDI outflow from Asia, followed by South Korea and Singapore.

While China is seen as drawing investments away from ASEAN, she is keen to promote bilateral trade and regional prosperity. In a speech at the 2003 ASEAN Business and Investment Summit by China's Premier of the State Council, Mr. Wen Jiabao, the importance of China-ASEAN bilateral relationship was emphasized. He noted that the region's abundant resources could provide for China's growing needs as she continues with rapid development, thereby offering her trading partners a bigger market and more opportunities for expansion. In 2004, China and ASEAN agreed to build up a free trade area (FTA) before 2010 which will boost the development of an economic region with 1.7 billion consumers, about US$1.8 trillion in GDP, and US$1.2 trillion in trade volume. The establishment of an FTA will make China ASEAN's third largest global trading region after the European Union and the North American Free Trade Zone. Other ASEAN FTAs under discussion are with the US, European Union, Japan, Korea, and India.

The vehicle to enhance the ASEAN business landscape by attracting investments and stimulating deeper regional cooperation is the Framework Agreement for the Integration of Priority Sectors and its Protocols. Eleven industry sectors were selected for development and integration on the basis of comparative advantage and contribution to the ASEAN economy. The priority sectors are shown in Table 3.3.

These sectors have their specific roadmaps and will enjoy special incentives such as zero internal tariffs, simplification and harmonization of standards and customs procedures, enhanced intellectual property rights (IPR) protection, and removal of all non-tariff barriers by 2010 or five years before Vision 2015. Active involvement of the private sector is expected to continue in these areas where high growth is projected for the coming years.

ASEAN businesses should tap into the initiatives and privileges given to companies based in this region. The opportunities will progressively increase and the markets will continue to expand. Companies

Table 3.3   ASEAN priority sectors

Goods and manufacturing	Services
Electronics	Infocomm technology (ICT) e-ASEAN
Wood-based products	Healthcare
Automotives	Air travel
Rubber-based products	Tourism
Textiles and apparels	
Agro-based products	
Fisheries	

planning to expand must think regional and regional companies must integrate globally by taking advantage of ASEAN's position and size. Local champions that continue to concentrate on the local market must explore options in the value chain to achieve cost-effectiveness. Strategic positioning involves analyzing the external business landscape, identifying the opportunities and threats, and recognizing the forces of change that impact the country, industry, and company. To stay competitive and ensure sustained growth in a globalized world, organizations must aim for global standards, maintain regional perspectives, and be local champions in the future ASEAN market.

Strategic marketing for a changing business landscape must apply a fundamental shift from an inside-out approach to one that uses an outside-in principle. The external environment is far more important in determining future consumer trends and markets, including competition and alliances. In addition, political directives and transnational initiatives such as ASEAN economic integration lends immeasurable assistance to organizations which take advantage of the incentives and schemes to promote trade and investments.

For businesses to participate and benefit in the economic growth in this region, a marketing strategy that embraces the goals and philosophies of the ASEAN Vision 2015 is a key success factor. The greatest impact that globalization brings about on ASEAN and any open economy for that matter is change.

Change is triggered mostly by external factors and technology has been the key driver for change in the history of globalization and world economic development. Change is a value migrator dependent on the certainty and importance of the change. It creates new demand and supply conditions. Organizations that respond timely and aptly to changes will survive and stand to emerge winners in a changing business landscape (see Figure 3.3). Organizations that are slow to react or complacent with their current situations will face totally different business conditions in which they are unable to fathom or penetrate due to the existence of established players in the marketplace.

Globalization is about going forward into the future. ASEAN and other regional blocs are already building the framework for future markets. Forward-looking organizations must work toward aligning themselves to this future globalized market where size is advantageous, economies of scale are vital, and technology is the key driver for

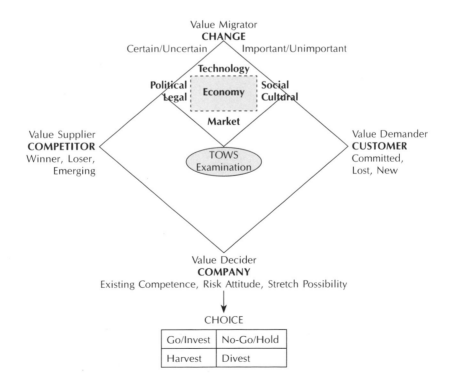

Figure 3.3　Business landscape configuration

productivity. The alternative is to be marginalized and gradually disappear in the dynamism of the new business landscape.

Open economies like ASEAN have to continuously adapt and adjust to external changes in order to take advantage of new opportunities and be prepared for new challenges. We use the comparison of the traditional and new economies shown earlier and adapt it to show the shift in norms and strategic focus for future businesses in today's evolving global economy (see Table 3.4).

Table 3.4   Changing business landscape

	Traditional businesses	Future businesses
Markets	National Overseas subject to tariffs	Trading bloc Free trade zones
Scope of competition	National (or regional) Protectionist	Global Liberalized
Organizational structure	Hierarchical Bureaucratic Specific Scope Localized	Networked Entrepreneurial Multidisciplinary Empowerment
Key productivity factor	Labor (skills) Capital In-house expertise Durability	Knowledge Innovation Outsourcing/Offshoring Time to market
Importance of research	Moderate Imitate and improve	Critical Innovate and invent
Nature of engagement	Mandate Relationship Intuition	Opportunistic Free market Due diligence
Regulation/ governance	Top-down silo Closed group	Connected matrix Transparency

Table 3.4—continued

Strategic management	Inside out—SWOT— strengths, weaknesses, opportunities, threats	Outside in—TOWS— threats, opportunities, weaknesses, strengths
Strategic marketing	3 Cs—customer, competition, company 4 Ps—product, place, promotion, pricing	4 Cs—change, customer, competition, company PDB triangle— positioning, differentiation, brand
Marketing focus	Product-centric Distribution	Customer-centric Service
Growth strategy	Market share	Sustainability

ASEAN's Future Market

Before we look into the crystal ball for a glimpse of the future, let us do an environmental scan of the world in general and ASEAN in particular. In 2004, the world economy grew by an average of 4% with developing countries—particularly China and India—enjoying robust performance. These new growth engines generate strong demand for raw materials and commodities, and as a result increase the import trade from resource-rich countries such as in ASEAN. With increasing flow of international trade, capital, information, and people, globalization facilitates proliferation of technologies that contributes to improved standards of living. The costs of technologies, transportation, and manufactured goods have been reducing due to more cost-effective and efficient methods of production and distribution. For example, the equivalent of today's US$1,000 computer was US$1.9 million in 1960. Lower transportation costs and an increasing need to do cross-border business set an uptrend for mobility and migration. On the downside, this exposes countries to the threats of terrorism, pandemics, and volatile markets.

Against a backdrop of natural and man-made calamities, escalating oil prices, and creeping interest rates, ASEAN has performed relatively well in recent years. In 2004 the region achieved an average economic growth rate of 5.8%, improved FDI of 22% despite a declining investment trend worldwide, and effectively managed a free trade zone with tariffs of 99% of products in the preferential inclusion list reduced to 0–5%. ASEAN's combined GDP of US$800 billion and two-way trade of US$1.05 trillion in 2004 make it the world's third largest trading bloc after EU and NAFTA, and the tenth highest in terms of GDP. Yet, individual ASEAN members may not make the ranks if each country tries to go it alone in the global market. Regional cooperation and global integration continue to play pivotal roles for ASEAN to be a formidable economic bloc in the age of globalization. ASEAN-5 will lead the group toward globalization and regional integration with Asia. Of the newer members, Vietnam has been showing consistent growth since it embarked on an economic reform package called *doi moi* ("renovation") in 1986 and since its entry into ASEAN in 1995.

ASEAN-5 belongs to the former 1990s "flying geese squadron" and has established long entrenched relationships with the world's largest economies and multinational corporations. With China's prominence as an economic giant, it has been debated if she will replace Japan as the "lead goose" in Asia. However, size is only one aspect of measurement of development. Industry lifecycles, competitiveness of capital- or technology-intensive industries, and product sophistication are major indicators of economic leadership. Although China has made impressive technological leapfrogs, her industries are predominantly low-to mid-tech such as textiles and household appliances. Japan (and maybe South Korea) is still the most advanced and dominant country in terms of sophistication and export structure with its high-tech electronics, optics, chemicals, and automobile industries, but it has lost a decade of progressive growth and technological leadership during its prolonged recession in the 1990s. At this moment technology transfer is not forthcoming from China. Will the "flying geese" formation take shape again? Our deduction is no.

Where does that place ASEAN?

Many lessons were learned in the last ten years. Asian countries that had depended on Japan to provide FDI and technology know-how have been forced to look elsewhere or within themselves for investments, trade, and technological advances. The regionalization efforts have become more pronounced. What we foresee as the future market of Asia and for ASEAN is the formation of squadrons of flying geese, each squadron made up of a single sizeable market comprising individual countries or a region. The new squadron formation will consist of Squadron Japan, Squadron China, Squadron Korea, Squadron SAARC (South Asian Association for Regional Cooperation), and Squadron ASEAN. These squadrons will create new markets of consumers, goods, and services by taking full advantage of liberalized trading conditions, digital connectivity and efficiency, and differentiating factors and dynamism. This concept in ASEAN has already gone beyond the "noise level" and various frameworks have been put in place to promote a vibrant and progressive free trade zone. The ASEAN future market is developing right here in its own region (see Table 3.5).

Table 3.5 Overview of ASEAN—Major industries, exports, and imports

Country	Major industries	Major exports	Major imports
Brunei	Oil and gas; textiles, food and beverages; building material	Oil and gas; ready-made garments	Transport equipment and machinery; manufactured goods; food; chemicals
Cambodia	Textiles and garments; beverages; food processing; tourism; rice milling; fisheries; rubber; cement; gem mining	Garments; textile products; sawn wood furniture; rubber	Transport equipment and machinery; manufactured goods; food; chemicals
Indonesia	Pulp and paper; cement; basic metals and fertilizer; power generation; telecommunications; transportation; rubber; food; tourism	Textiles; electronic goods; footwear; oil and gas; plywood; sawn timber	Chemicals and pharmaceuticals; fertilizer; cotton yarns; textile fabric; machines; motor vehicles

Table 3.5—continued

Laos	Garments; wood-based and processing; cement; electricity; copper; tin; gypsum mining; agricultural processing; construction; tourism	Coffee; electricity; clothing; wood and forest products; gypsum	Industrial machinery; chemicals; iron; electrical machinery and parts; steel; oil; construction material; consumption goods
Malaysia	Electronic and electrical goods; textiles; clothing and footwear; chemicals; petroleum production and refining; wood and metal products; rubber; oil palm; light manufacturing; agricultural processing; logging	Electronic and electrical machinery; petroleum and LNG; textiles, clothing and footwear; palm oil; sawn timber	Manufacturing inputs; machinery and transport equipment; metal products
Myanmar	Agro-based products; textiles; steel, copper, tin, tungsten, iron; construction materials; pharmaceuticals; fertilizer; cement; natural gas	Rice; teak; beans and pulses; rubber; coffee; minerals; gems; marine products	Power tillers; hand tractors; fertilizer; diesel oil; cement; dumper, loader, and spare parts; water pumps; hydraulic excavator
Philippines	Construction material; electronics; food; giftware and holiday décor; home furnishings; IT and IT-enabled services; marine products; motor vehicle parts and components; organic and natural products; wearables; petroleum refining; fishery	Electronic products; garments; ignition and other wiring sets used in vehicles, aircraft, and ships; coconut oil; bananas; woodcraft and furniture; manufactured products; petroleum products; metal components; cathodes and sections of cathodes of refined copper	Electronic products; mineral fuels, lubricants, and related materials; industrial machinery and equipment; transport equipment; iron and steel; cereal and cereal preparations; textile yarn; fabrics; made-up articles and related products; telecommunications equipment and electricity machinery; plastics in primary and

Table 3.5—continued

			non-primary forms; organic and non-organic chemicals
Singapore	Electronics; chemicals; banking and finance; real estate; tourism; trading; oil drilling equipment; petroleum refining; rubber processing and products; processed food and beverages; ship repair; offshore platform construction; life sciences	Petroleum products; industrial machines; radio and television receivers and parts; electronic components and parts; clothing; beverages and tobacco	Crude petroleum; iron and steel; industrial machines; electric generators; electronic components and parts
Thailand	Electronics; gems and jewelry; footwear; textiles; clothing; tourism; agricultural processing; beverages; tobacco; cement; computers and parts; integrated circuits; furniture; plastics; automobiles and automotive parts; tungsten and tin	Textiles; computers and components; integrated circuits and parts; gems and jewelry; footwear	Industrial machinery; iron and steel; electrical machinery and parts; chassis and body
Vietnam	Agriculture; forestry; fishery; industrial construction; food processing; garments; footwear; machine building; mining; coal; steel; cement; fertilizer; glass; tires; oil; paper	Crude oil; coal; chromium; tin; cement; woolen and jute carpets; rice; cinnamon; marine products	Motors; petroleum products; diesel oil; fertilizer

Source: ASEAN Secretariat and *CIA World Factbook*.

To realize the full potential of ASEAN, all countries must be viewed as a single region. ASEAN members stand to benefit tremendously from the expanded scope and size that the entire group offers to each other and to the world with the lifting of tariffs and non-tariff barriers by 2010; harmonization of product standards and conformity assessment procedures; liberalization of investments for ASEAN and non-ASEAN investors; establishment of a dispute settlement mechanism; and fast-tracking the integration process of 11 priority sectors. Using the Morgan Stanley Capital International (MSCI) Global Industry Classification Standard (GICS), we construct an ASEAN profile (see Table 3.6) to show the comparative advantages and potential for each country and industry sector from which we can map out the future market for the region.

Table 3.6   Comparative advantages and potential for ASEAN countries by sector

Industry sector	Coverage	Focus industries in countries
Energy—oil and gas	Drilling, exploration, production, equipment, services, refining and marketing, storage and transportation	Brunei, Indonesia, Malaysia, Philippines, Singapore, Vietnam
Materials	Chemicals, construction material, containers, packaging, metals and mining, paper and forest products	Cambodia, Indonesia, Laos, Malaysia, Myanmar, Philippines, Thailand, Vietnam

Table 3.6—continued

Industrials	Aerospace and defense, building products, construction and engineering, electrical equipment machinery, trading companies, distributors, commercial services and supplies, air freight and logistics, airlines, marine, road, rail, transportation infrastructure	
Consumer discretionary	Auto components and automobiles, household durables, leisure equipment and products, textiles, apparel and luxury goods, hotels, restaurants and leisure, diversified consumer services, media, retail	Cambodia, Indonesia, Malaysia, Philippines, Thailand, Singapore, Vietnam
Consumer staples	Food and staples, beverages and food products, tobacco, household and personal products	Cambodia, Indonesia, Laos, Malaysia, Myanmar, Philippines, Thailand, Singapore, Vietnam
Healthcare	Equipment and supplies, providers and services, technology, biotechnology, pharmaceuticals, life sciences	Indonesia, Malaysia, Thailand, Singapore
Financials	Commercial banks, thrift and mortgage finance, consumer finance, capital markets, insurance, real estate investment, management and development	Indonesia, Malaysia, Philippines, Thailand, Singapore

Table 3.6—continued

Information technology	Software, services, computer equipment and peripherals, electronic equipment and instruments, office electronics, semiconductors	Indonesia, Malaysia, Philippines, Thailand, Singapore
Telecommunications	Equipment and services	Indonesia, Malaysia, Philippines, Thailand, Singapore
Utilities	Electricity, gas, water	Indonesia, Malaysia, Philippines, Thailand, Singapore

The future market for ASEAN is intra-ASEAN among the ten countries, and extra-ASEAN with the traditional trading partners: the US; EU; Japan; growing economies; China, India, and South Korea; and other global open economies. The greatest potential for growth are those industries that contribute to free flow of goods and services such as transportation, and in areas where ASEAN has a clear comparative advantage such as high-tech manufacturing and ICT (see Table 3.7).

For example, the logistics sector is set to grow rapidly with the liberalization of markets and removal of tariffs in ASEAN. This potentially lucrative business is especially needed in the newly opened economies of Cambodia, Laos, Myanmar, and Vietnam, as well as Indonesia and the Philippines where the geographies are relatively stretched. Developing an efficient logistics network will require construction of roads, ports and storage facilities, transportation, handling expertise, and the entire supply chain of material, people, skills, and equipment. Japanese automobile manufacturers have committed to making ASEAN their R&D and production centers

Table 3.7 ASEAN—Existing and future markets by industry sector

Industry sector	Focus industries in countries	Existing markets	Future markets
Energy—oil and gas	Brunei, Indonesia, Malaysia, Philippines, Singapore, Vietnam	US, EU, Japan	ASEAN, global
Materials	Cambodia, Indonesia, Laos, Malaysia, Myanmar, Philippines, Thailand, Vietnam	US, EU, Japan	ASEAN, global
Industrials	Indonesia, Malaysia, Philippines, Singapore, Thailand	US, EU, Japan	ASEAN, global
Consumer discretionary	Cambodia, Indonesia, Malaysia, Philippines, Thailand, Singapore, Vietnam	US, EU, Japan	ASEAN, global
Consumer staples	Cambodia, Indonesia, Laos, Malaysia, Myanmar, Philippines, Thailand, Singapore, Vietnam	Domestic, US, EU, Japan	ASEAN, global
Healthcare	Indonesia, Malaysia, Philippines, Thailand, Singapore	Domestic	ASEAN, global
Financials	Indonesia, Malaysia, Philippines, Thailand, Singapore	Domestic	ASEAN, Islamic countries
Information technology	Indonesia, Malaysia, Philippines, Thailand, Singapore	US, EU, Japan	ASEAN, global

Table 3.7—continued

Telecommunications	Indonesia, Malaysia, Philippines, Thailand, Singapore	US, EU, Japan	ASEAN, global
Utilities	Indonesia, Malaysia, Philippines, Thailand, Singapore	Domestic	ASEAN

for auto parts and full assembly of vehicles. The Chairman of Japan Automobile Manufacturers Association (JAMA), Mr. Itaru Koeda, cited in his speech in Malaysia in May 2005 that with Japan's cooperation for an expanded market in Asia, the elimination of tariffs is a clear advantage for ASEAN to become competitive globally.

ASEAN's future market is right here on its own home turf. The winners are those who establish themselves in these markets and the losers are the latecomers and those who do not expand regionally. Its largest trading partners are beginning to refocus their investments and businesses in this region. The top five countries in 2003 that invested in ASEAN were the UK (17.3%), Netherlands (15.5%), the US (15%), Japan (10.6%), and Singapore (6.7%). Brunei was the main receiver of FDI from the UK and the Netherlands as part of oil exploration and petroleum-related projects. Singapore received the most FDI from the US, followed by Malaysia, mainly in the IT-related industries. Japan's FDI was highest in Thailand particularly in the automobile industry. The top FDI recipients in 2003 were Singapore (56%), Brunei (15%), Malaysia (10%), Thailand (9%), and Vietnam (7%). It is interesting to note that while Japan, ASEAN's top Asian business partner, invested more in China in absolute dollars, the bulk of the investment was in the Chinese manufacturing sector. FDI in non-manufacturing industries such as transport, electrical goods and electronics, food, and chemicals in ASEAN was 40% higher than Japan's FDI in China.

With an ASEAN free trade zone and more free trade areas being agreed on with other regions, businesses here must adopt a globalized approach for economic integration and maximization of comparative advantages. For example, a Malaysian fashion designer may source fabric from Thailand, hand-make the dresses in Laos, and sell them in Paris and New York. Similarly, an MNC may set its production base in Indonesia with raw materials from Cambodia, Myanmar, and Vietnam, employ Singaporean managers, implement inventory software from the Philippines, and supply manufactured equipment to Brunei and Dubai.

This is already happening and many successful companies are doing business in this manner. The biggest change today is the expanded and evolving playing field. Local companies should seek to extend their businesses into neighboring markets similar to their own countries' while using competencies developed at home. Multinational companies should tap into the comparative advantages available in ASEAN as a production and R&D base as well as target the region's large consumer market. Globalization presents a vast amount of opportunities and potential, as well as threats and complexities. Regionalization is the direction to take.

Compete for ASEAN Customers

With the world becoming more and more globalized, individual countries have to liberalize their markets in order to stay internationally competitive.[1]

Lim Chong Yah

Andy Grove, the former CEO of Intel Corporation, wrote in his book *Only the Paranoid Survive:* "You have to be willing to eat your own young." Although this may sound rather morbid and revolting, it revealed how the world's microprocessor giant was its own biggest competitor by becoming the single source of successor models for the Intel 8086 microprocessor when it came under pressure from cheaper Japanese-made microchips. That was back in the early 1980s and Intel has since become one of the world's most recognized brands and mega successes.

However, with globalization and the convergence of infocomm technologies, competition will not always come in traditional packages. In future, Intel's competitors may not necessarily come from only microprocessor chip manufacturers but possibly from mobile phone, consumer electronics, or Internet gaming companies. Similarly, in the service industry, airlines are not only competing with other airlines for business travelers. Instead, airline competitors may come in the form of advanced teleconferencing, instant document exchange, online sampling, and virtually any digitized business services and transactions. Waiting in line to be screened at the airport and lugging equipment and material from one place to another may be a thing of the past.

---

[1] Lim Chong Yah, *Southeast Asia: The Long Road Ahead,* Second edition. Singapore: World Scientific Publishing Co. Ltd, 2004.

Multimode, hyperspeed transmission of data, image, and voice (and perhaps in the future simulated scents and touch) will allow executives to conduct personal and effective meetings with anyone anywhere in the world, as many times a day as needed.

In previous chapters we emphasized change as the value migrator and the major influence in shaping the competition and future consumer markets. New entrants into the competitive space will not only be the typical companies producing the same products and services competing for the same or different market segments. Businesses must not only analyze and monitor the known competitors. In *Competing for the Future*, Hamel and Prahalad highlighted that if businesses were to control their markets, they must compete for the future. It is not enough for them just to think about current conditions, competitors, or customers, let alone those in the past. Everything important is in the future and the ability to prepare for it is crucial.

In our book, *Rethinking Marketing: Sustainable Market-ing Enterprise in Asia*, three dimensions are identified to analyze competitors. The first dimension—the general dimension—refers to the typical general profile of existing and potential competitors and providers of substitute products and services. The second dimension—the aggressive dimension—looks at the extent to which competitors implement creative and aggressive strategies by building on competitive advantages of price and quality; timing and know-how; and a strong market position. The third dimension—the capability dimension—is about competing on capabilities of financial strength, and tangible and intangible assets.

As ASEAN heads toward a more liberalized business environment, competition will be more intensified with an increasing number of players entering the market. Local companies will have to contend with regional or international competitors instead of the competitor across the road. Businesses that lack competitive advantages will find it difficult to survive if they are unable to fight off aggressive competition. Forward-looking companies which had anticipated this situation would have taken steps to regionalize, reinvent, or diversify their businesses.

An example is the Filipino Goldilocks Bake and Food Shop that has successfully served the uniquely *Pinoy* taste and continues to add new concepts like it has done for the past 39 profitable years despite the intrusion of copycats and foreign competition.

Proactive companies that compete for the future will perform better and stay longer than reactive companies that strive only for the present. A proactive company must take change seriously as an important factor in defining its strategies. Strategic choices in turn impact on the future of the company. Changes in technological advances, political policies, economic development, and social-cultural behaviors will cascade to the business environment where new competitors are drawn in while others may disappear, and changing customer profiles and behaviors will dictate changes in needs for products and services.

ASEAN Vision, Local Action

In the earlier chapters, we have described the changing political and economic environment of doing business in ASEAN. The shift to global integration, diffusion of infocomm technologies, and the focus on regionalization are the forces of change and key growth drivers in ASEAN. As of January 1, 2005 tariffs on 98.98% of the products in the Common Effective Preferential Tariff (CEPT) Inclusion List (IL) of ASEAN-6 have been reduced to the 0–5% tariff range.[2] This translates to freer movement of goods, services, labor, and capital from one country to another. Although there are signs of export recovery with traditional foreign trading partners, intra-ASEAN trade remained stagnant. More must be done to motivate the domestic small and medium-sized companies to regionalize and create ASEAN as a single market.

Competition for ASEAN customers will only get more intense as the region opens up. China-made goods and Indian software will

---

[2] ASEAN Annual Report 2004/2005. ASEAN-6 refers to ASEAN-5 members and Brunei Darussalam.

continue to penetrate the markets. Multinationals and government-linked regional corporations with strong financial and intellectual capabilities provide investments as well as competition in domestic industries. For example, Malaysia's evolving retail industry shows that traditional convenience and neighborhood stores are losing to the Western-style hypermarket shopping experience provided by big global players such as Tesco and Carrefour. 31% of urban Malaysian shoppers turn to these hypermarkets as their main shopping destinations. In order to stay competitive in this saturated market, all local retailers have no choice but to alter their business tactics to keep up.[3]

Authors Niraj Dawar and Tony Frost share the various options that local companies can have when competing in the face of the vast financial and technological resources, the seasoned management, and the powerful global brands.[4] These options are dependent on the strength of globalization pressures in an industry and the nature of a company's competitive assets. The strategic options for local companies competing with multinationals in emerging markets are known as defender, extender, dodger, and contender options.

Where globalization pressures are low, a local company may be able to defend its market share by leveraging the advantages it enjoys in its home market by defending or extending its business depending on its competitive assets. If globalization pressures are high, a local company can either dodge or contend for its market share. When a company's competitive assets are customized to the home market, it will have to dodge into a locally oriented link within the value chain, or enter into merger and acquisition deals with other companies. A contending company aims to compete directly with multinationals for global customers by focusing

---

[3] "Retailing in Malaysia," *Euromonitor International*, June 2004.

[4] Niraj Dawar and Tony Frost, "Competing with the Giants: Survival Strategies for Local Companies in Emerging Markets," *Harvard Business Review*, 1999.

on upgrading capabilities and resources. An example is Creative Technology's Zen competing with Apple's iPod for the digital music player market.

It is inevitable that competition in ASEAN will get more intense. Local enterprises must explore and learn to exploit the advantages of regional and global integration, and continuously reassess their competitive position. For example, Singapore has been successful in wooing medical visitors, especially wealthy Indonesians, to its sophisticated and renowned specialist clinics and hospitals for many years. When the financial crisis hit Indonesia, Singapore's medical business dropped significantly. In the meantime, Thailand's medico-tourism was winning customers with their low fees and no waiting sales pitches while rising costs pushed Singapore to invest in hospitals in relatively cheaper Malaysia.

Where markets become saturated in certain industries, regionalization and offshoring are potentially viable strategies. We say "potentially" because companies seeking new markets overseas must carefully consider local environments and business landscapes in order to succeed. Superficially all markets for the same type of products and services appear the same. Probe deeper and subtle differences will become apparent. A good illustration is the automobile market. When Toyota started its first offshore plant in Indonesia in 1971, it studied the local road and traffic conditions, family configurations and affordability, and driving preferences, and localized its design to produce the four-wheel-drive minivan *Kijang* which has remained the bestselling car in Indonesia for almost 30 years. If Toyota had continued to produce and market the same type of saloon models popular in other countries, it may not have been successful in being the top automobile brand that meets the Indonesian needs and suits the local driving environment.

Multinational corporations (MNCs) with their broader scopes and larger worldwide operations have to constantly assess their competencies to maintain global standards and localized market conditions to meet different customer demands in different countries. Striking a balance between global standardization and local effectiveness is a delicate exercise for many MNCs. Theodore Levitt elaborated on his highly debated rationale of global standardization by dismissing the future of MNCs, arguing that they would be completely absorbed by global corporations.[5] He predicted that globalization would "break the walls of economic insularity, nationalism, and chauvinism" making the world a market where people have the same desires and lifestyles. According to him, this was the result of technology which determines human preferences and globalization which enables economic realities, making global markets homogeneous and served by low-cost standardized goods and services. Hindsight evaluation concurs that his views may be too extreme in painting the impact of globalization on MNCs.

Drawing from Levitt's perspectives of strategy for global companies, we ascertain that the best approach for companies focusing on ASEAN is *glorecalization* or globalization of values, regionalization of strategies, and localization of tactics. This translates to our strategic business triangle of brand, positioning, and differentiation and our 3C formula. The first "C" stands for consistent global value which represents the company's brand, service, and process. All three elements should be standardized due to the high cost and investment in development. The second "C" is the coordinated regional strategy consisting of segmentation, targeting, and positioning. This takes into consideration the differences and similarities of consumers in different countries and devising appropriate strategies for the target markets. The third "C" is about customized local tactic whereby the company differentiates itself from competitors, and applies a suitable set of marketing mix and selling techniques.

To implement glorecalization successfully, companies must bear in mind that the ASEAN market is at different development stages and has diverse cultures, languages, demographics, income levels, geographical sizes, and technological advances. The ten-nation free trade region with a combined population of over 540 million

---

[5] Theodore Levitt, "The Globalization of Markets," *Harvard Business Review*, 1983.

represents a sizeable consumer market larger than the entire European Union (456 million) and US (298 million). Competing for ASEAN customers requires a good understanding of the ASEAN customer's buying motivations and restrictions, product choices, and most importantly, the needs arising from desires and anxieties that are both obvious and covert. Without first understanding the ASEAN customer, it will not be easy to achieve exceptional results from any winning formula.

Understanding ASEAN Customers

A typical approach in understanding customers is to define a profile by way of segmentation. Geographic segmentation divides the market into geographical units such as country and region, culture and language, and urban and rural. Demographic segmentation divides the market according to gender, age, occupation, religion, race, and education. Psychographic segmentation focuses on lifestyles, attitudes, values, and beliefs. Behavioral segmentation profiles consumer brand loyalty and product usage (heavy, regular, or occasional).

In a globalized world, these segments are inclined to shift easily and get finely blended because people, technology, and capital move faster and more freely. As a result, segmentation becomes very difficult to define and customer profiling based on lagged statistical and analytical reports will not be meaningful at best and at worst, extremely risky as input for strategic planning.

A study of future retail banking trends, The Paradox of Banking 2015, by the IBM Institute of Business Value, reported that customer demand will transform from a bell curve to a well curve where a majority of customers being served more or less similar products today will move to the extremes of the product spectrum by demanding either low-cost mass-market products or high-value targeted financial instruments. The conclusive forces of change are increasing customer diversity, infocomm technologies access, and pronounced shifts in demographics and value systems. These changes create well-informed, hands-on, and more discerning consumers who will not

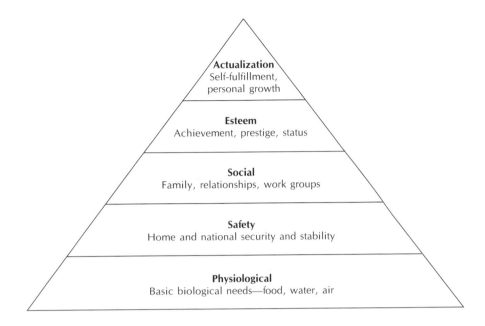

Figure 4.1   Maslow's hierarchy of needs

hesitate to demand for greater advocacy and control in their banking relationships.

Maslow's hierarchy of needs (see Figure 4.1) is often referred to when studying market segments and customer profiles. We use this to demonstrate the ASEAN customer base with relation to the different development stages of the member countries.

At a national level, the primary role of a government is to provide for the fundamental physiological and safety needs of the people. This was very evident in post-war Southeast Asian countries. As a country progresses economically, the pursuit of quality of life, freedom of choices, and wealth accumulation become more prevalent. Once a country achieves tangible material goals, it seeks for a level of accomplishment for *meta-needs*, which as Maslow explained, cannot be permanently satiated. These needs are linked to the search for truth, beauty, goodness, perfection, and often associated with the arts, heritage, and religion. Maslow's hierarchy of needs can also be mapped to the economic and social development in Daniel Pink's *A Whole*

New Mind which compared the effects of technology advancement to human evolution of the primitive hunter that evolves to the farmer, then to the blue-collar worker, progresses to a white-collar executive, and finally to an artist or arts patron.

In economic terms, the hunter (or fisherman) represents the lowest income group depending on subsistence living and having little or no technological access. The farmer represents the second lowest income group belonging to the agriculural, forestry, or mining sectors with limited bargaining powers and caught at the bottom of a value chain filled with cartels, government bureaucracy, and internationally controlled markets. The blue-collar worker, who has one or more technical skills in machine operation, factory assembly, or industrial production, is paid regular wages and given employment welfare. The white-collar executive or office worker reflects the educated, professional labor force in the services sector such as finance, IT, healthcare, retail, travel, and education. This group enjoys high income and career advancement prospects, is technologically savvy, and displays the strongest consumerism culture. The artist or art patron portrays the super-rich and ultra-successful group at the pinnacle of society that yearns for things that money cannot buy.

Depending on a country's technological advancement and economic development, all five classifications exist in some ASEAN countries while in others only three or four groups are dominant. As mentioned in Chapter 1, the infostate level is an indicator of a country's progress and the concentration of ICT activities is observed in places where people have achieved material comfort, knowledge, and status. The infostate or infocomm technologies development level is another important consideration when profiling the ASEAN customer (see Figure 4.2).

ASEAN consumers in general have transformed from simple buyers of basic necessities to sophisticated consumers with higher disposable incomes, better education, improved health conditions and consciousness, and broader international outlooks arising from greater access to information and modern communications. Karthik Siva, the founding chairman of Global Brand Forum and Group Strategy

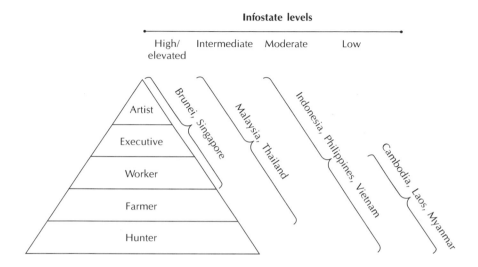

Figure 4.2　Infostate development levels

Director of Ogilvy and Mather Singapore, argued that there are new realities and challenges facing Asian consumers in general, and ASEAN consumers in particular. The most pronounced factor is the Asian aspiration to be modern and progressive, but not necessarily Western. As diverse and heterogeneous as Asia is, there exists a common set of values for harmony and order, institution above individual, respect for elders, strong family and community ties, fear of losing face and honor, team above self, consensus-based approach, strong traditional anchors, and premium on relationships rather than objectivity. This observation is crucial especially for companies expanding regionally or multinationals doing business in ASEAN.

Siva suggested that there are two solutions to reaching out to Asian customers. The first solution is to leverage universal human insights but localize them to fit a country. The second is an ethnocentric localized approach that disregards globalization completely. McDonald's, known internationally by its golden arches and tasty burgers, uses its universal advertising campaign of talking to parents through children. Yet it does not use a standardized commercial worldwide. Instead, every country has different commercials with its local sense of value and humor. On top of that, McDonald's makes efforts to serve burgers to suit local tastes and cultures such as the non-beef Maharaja Mac available only in India where the cow is considered a sacred animal, and there are no hamburgers in all Muslim countries.

There is of course no stereotype ASEAN customer and no single secret formula in understanding ASEAN customers. Surface appearances do not reveal the deep-rooted human insights of the ASEAN consumer. Western-style dressing does not necessarily mean Western thinking. For example, a cheongsam-clad Caucasian lady is immediately noticeable in a crowd while a Chinese man in a business suit speaking English mingles inconspicuously. It is safe to conclude that the lady does not conform to Confucian values but tough to figure out if the man is a Buddhist, Christian, or Muslim. Understanding ASEAN customers is a bigger challenge compared to customers in racially homogeneous markets like Japan, Korea, and China. However, without first understanding ASEAN customers, it will be an uphill task to compete successfully with the local champions and established foreign players.

Understanding ASEAN customers is not only about measuring GDP or infostates, although such information provides good indications of segmentation and affordability levels. The deeper and more difficult-to-extract characteristics are the elusive ASEAN customer anxieties and desires. These needs are not obvious, not openly discussed, and sometimes not known to the customers themselves. For example, in Singapore, the three main races—Chinese, Malay, and Indian—have very different values, social expectations, and concerns. The Chinese are generally industrious, pragmatic, and materialistic. The Malays hold principals of rustic simplicity, an unhurried approach to life, family orientation, community living, and graciousness. The Indians in general value spirituality, family honor, intellectual orientation, and respect for elders. Local companies going ASEAN have more advantage in understanding this aspect than MNCs establishing themselves in this region, and winning strategies can only be formulated once ASEAN customers are correctly understood.

Competing in the New Business Landscape

Throughout this book, we highlighted the 4 "Cs"—Change, Competitor, Customer, and Company—as key considerations in strategic management. Change brought about by technological, political, economic, or social transformations will create new "rules of the (business) game." These rules could be in the form of trade liberation, mandatory use of electronic tax filing, or policy to create elderly-friendly facilities. We look at change as a value migrator that fuels two distinct reactions, future supply and demand, which in turn defines the new competitor and customer profiles respectively.

Markets are either supply-driven or demand-driven (see Figure 4.3). An example of a supply-driven market is the mobile phone market

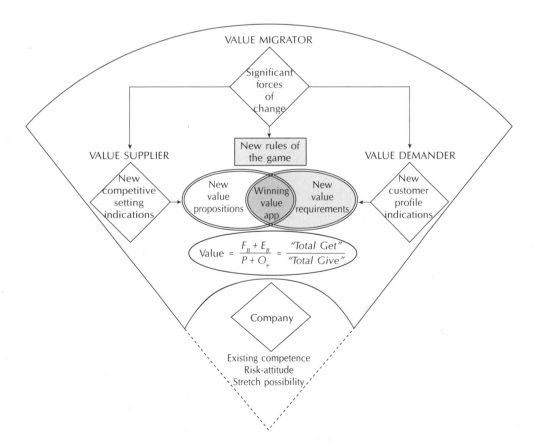

Figure 4.3   The new landscape configuration

where the cost of mobile phones and the accessibility to mobile networks have been made so affordable that high consumer adoption continues to support the underlying demand. On the other hand, an example of demand-driven market is the automobile industry where the demand for cars is derived primarily from the rise in affluence as a result of economic growth in a country. From the two examples, one can deduce that the change driver in the mobile phone market is technology, and the change driver in the automobile market is economy.

The winning value application is one which matches the new value requirement with the new value proposition. This value is represented by the functional and emotional benefits that the customer receives in return for paying the cost of acquiring the product or service. A company aiming to achieve winning value applications in a pervasively changing environment will have to study its existing competence, risk attitude, and stretch possibility. Competency is the capability to perform to requirements using existing resources and to procure new resources when needed. Risk attitude is the ability to overcome uncertainties and unforeseen circumstances to accomplish novel innovations, explore fresh markets, and lead new changes. Stretch possibility is the stamina and agility to sustain the business growth when entry to a market may be too early or affected by uncontrollable events such as natural disasters that may derail plans.

Competing in an evolving business landscape demands a clear understanding of your customers' needs and their reactions to changes. Essentially the most important elements in winning ASEAN customers are to endorse global standards, maintain regional perspectives, and be local champions for their products and services. A company's orientation to enable its competitive strategy is dependent on its overall management strategy and corporate direction. In 1969 Dr. Howard V. Perlmutter, a pioneer of globalization strategy studies, put forward the theory that there are four company orientations (known as EPRG) to explain the evolutionary and competitive outlooks of different companies.

The first orientation is ethnocentric (E) where the focus is on the home country which is considered superior and to which other countries should strive to emulate. Ethnocentric or "domestic" companies are less likely to expand locally or overseas as they see themselves successful enough in their own territories. The second, polycentric (P) orientation accepts that every country has different characteristics and sees the host country as unique. Polycentric or "multinational" companies understand that conditions are not the same as in their home country and the management of operations needs to be adjusted to suit the host countries. The third type of orientation is regiocentric (R) where both differences and similarities are considered. Regiocentric or "regional" companies are ethnocentric in thinking and polycentric in execution. The fourth, geocentric (G) orientation sees the world in its entirety with differences and similarities as a single target. Transnational or global companies adopt geocentric orientation and develop one integrated strategy for the whole world.

The long-term survival of a company is dependent on its orientation and strategic approach to its customers and competitors. Ethnocentric companies are in danger of being sandwiched by local and regional competitors. Often the survivability of such companies is due to government protection or tariffs which will be under tremendous pressure for annihilation in an increasingly globalized world, in which case, the ethnocentric companies may cease to exist. The most commonly found company orientations are polycentric and regiocentric. At the other extreme, geocentric-oriented companies with a single strategy for the whole world will likely find many failures and difficulties in competing with local or regional companies.

In his controversial book *The End of Globalization*,[6] Alan Rugman was adamant that the geocentric company is a myth as it is impossible to offer a completely disparate world a single solution. As the world has become a complex interconnected multicultural

---

[6] Alan Rugman, *The End of Globalization*. Random House Business Books, 2000.

system, it is unwise to isolate one type of orientation to determine a company strategy. A company may have polycentric human resource management, regiocentric marketing, and geocentric service quality. An example of positive amalgamation of orientations is HSBC, one of the largest banking and financial services organizations in the world with an international network of over 9,500 offices in 76 countries. Headquartered in London, the bank serves 31 million customers globally. To communicate its philosophy of having a worldwide experience with world-class service while respecting the local cultures and people, HSBC adopted a simple but powerful four-word slogan "The World's Local Bank." In Malaysia, the bank uses a Malay tagline, "*Bank Sedunia Memahami Hasrat Setempat,*" which implies "a global bank that understands local needs." For four consecutive years, the bank was awarded the title Global Bank of the Year (2002–2005)—a strong testament of its successful implementation of "Think Global, Act Local" strategy.

Companies that "think ASEAN" must act local in order to compete effectively. BreadTalk, the Singapore-based bakery boutique, has been expanding to other ASEAN cities. To compete with domestic confectionery shops, BreadTalk offers local flavored breads paying close attention to *halal* (Muslim) and other special requirements. In Thailand, AirAsia goes by the name Thai AirAsia and in Indonesia it is known as Indonesia AirAsia. The presence of Vietnamese Pho24 noodle restaurants, Indonesian Es Teller 77 restaurants, and Thai Black Canyon coffeehouses in ASEAN cities outside their home countries is indicative of regional interest by local companies. Local companies have the advantage when it comes to expanding into ASEAN markets because it is easier for them to identify the similarities and differences between their home and host countries. Having been in the same neighborhood, these companies understand the unique conditions of the host countries and are able to apply suitable approaches for their target markets.

The forces of change have created new rules of the game as ASEAN-thinking companies establish themselves in the region. To gain competitive advantage, companies must adopt local action, understand ASEAN customers, and integrate fully with regional markets. Competing for ASEAN customers is about competing in a changing business landscape in a fast-developing regional ASEAN market that is gradually opening up for greater regionalization and globalization.

In the next section, we select some local, regional, and multinational companies to discuss why and how they have been successful in ASEAN and to draw lessons from these companies on how they have competed for ASEAN customers.

Part II

Lessons from ASEAN Marketing Companies

Every organization in the world must have its own unique mission which is also the fundamental reason for its existence. This mission may change from time to time with organizational changes or external environment factors that force the organization to change its mission in order to survive. A mission translates into the value that an organization gives to its customers who in turn develop the value in its name and identification of its brand. The mission defines why an organization exists.

To determine what values will be delivered to its customers, strategic marketing concepts must be employed. This involves the analysis of target markets, competitive conditions, and internal resources to formulate a strategy to position the organization's brand, products, and services in the minds of the customers. Positioning is about promising the delivery of a specific value set and the organization's responsibility to its customers. It is the process of building credibility and brand integrity.

Finally, the organization must perform the actual delivery by carefully choosing the tactics of how its products and services can be received by customers. The success of this process will differentiate an organization from its competitors in terms of content (what to offer), context (how to offer), and infrastructure (the enabler of content and context, i.e., technology, people, and facilities). Differentiation is about how an organization applies the understanding of its customers' needs to satisfy their desires.

The positioning-differentiation-brand triangle is one of the most important marketing tools that link the relationship between an organization's mission, vision, and strategy. It is the basis of every success in business. Without this relationship, an organization will be drifting directionless and be lost, battled out by competitors, or simply become irrelevant amid rapid technological changes.

The three core elements of the strategic business triangle are interlinked and work seamlessly as one self-reinforcing mechanism. The process is self-repeating and increases in magnitude until it reaches a point where it snowballs, creating either a phenomenal success or a vicious downward spiral. When applied early in an organization's life, the strategic business triangle will create a strong foundation to build competitive advantages and brand values in the present and future markets. Branding is no longer about advertising and public communications. It is more about an organization's overall efforts to win the customers' trust, loyalty, and conviction in its brand, and to avoid presenting its products and services like commodities.

In the next three chapters, you will find excellent working models of companies which have used the positioning-differentiation-brand triangle successfully to market their brands. These companies are leaders in their own niche markets or industries, all sharing the same principle of making their customers feel special.

chapter 5

Watch out for the Local Champions

Giants—"new tech," CRM, etc. notwithstanding—will always be clumsy and impersonal relative to an "intimate local" who is really out to make a dramatic difference.[1]

Tom Peters

Home-grown businesses are effectively the toughest niche players in any marketplace. Large multinationals are usually less worried about their peer competitors because they have somewhat the same business models and therefore usually apply similar strategies. Armed with sophisticated systems and internationally standardized products, business giants tend to face culture shocks and blocks when it comes to serving local niche markets. On the other hand, the small domestic players are extremely agile in meeting the local customers' needs which are difficult to predict, and therefore almost unbeatable in the markets that they are entrenched.

What then are the winning strategies of these local champions that command the respect and loyalty of customers in a market where consumers are spoilt for choice by the wide range of products and services? How do successful local brands continue to do well in a globalized and highly competitive environment? The common thread found in these local companies is one of preserving traditions and staying relevant to the times. Such practices etch into the corporate culture and build distinctive brands, perfect positioning, and exclusive differentiation. The following case studies demonstrate clearly the strategic business core elements of positioning, differentiation, and

---

[1] "Beating Wal-Mart (Starbucks, etc.) Is a Lark!" Tom Peters blog, http://www/tompeters.com.

branding of these local champions in diverse industries ranging from food and beverage to medical and finance.

We have selected six interesting companies that are well recognized in their respective niche markets and have earned the indisputable "top-of-mind" brands in their own countries. In this chapter, we present the stories behind the successes of Bengawan Solo from Singapore, Dji Sam Soe from Indonesia, Goldilocks from the Philippines, MBF Cards from Malaysia, Bangkok Hospital from Thailand, and Number One Tonic Drink from Vietnam. Each of these companies shares a similar philosophy—providing the best for their customers with the use of local resources and know-how to satisfy their unique tastes, desires, and preferences.

Let us begin with the case of Bengawan Solo.

Bengawan Solo

Home-made *nyonya kueh* (Peranakan cakes) were once only found in Singapore's morning markets. Premium local cakes and pastries used to be available only during festive seasons like Chinese New Year and Hari Raya Puasa. Enter Anastasia Liew, an Indonesian married to a Singaporean, with a passion for baking. The illustrious housewife began making delicious Indonesian delicacies to entertain her friends and relatives at home and whenever she visited them. Word of her mouth-watering desserts and snacks went round and informal orders poured in. Before long, Anastasia was preparing tasty cakes in her own kitchen for friends, friends of friends, and even for some local supermarkets. Operating without a food manufacturing license, Anastasia's home business was soon discovered and stopped by the Ministry of Environment.

Not wanting to disappoint her customers, Anastasia set up a proper food company in 1979 and started Bengawan Solo Cake Shop, the first modern traditional *kueh* confectionery. Once considered a "dying" trade when Western-style cake shops were becoming popular among young people in Singapore, the art of making traditional cakes was revitalised by Bengawan Solo. Local customs involve presentation of gifts on special occasions such as weddings, a baby's first-month celebration, and other festive occasions. Often traditional *kueh* is part of the gift. Bengawan Solo understood these customary practices and became well patronized by loyal customers who continue to buy its cakes for their own consumption as well as gifts for others.

Starting from the kitchen at the back of a small shophouse in the heartland area, the company's central kitchen has now expanded to a 25,000 square foot factory serving 38 retail outlets around the island, with an annual sales turnover exceeding S$30million. Over 100 traditional and new "innovative-traditional" recipes are available all year round. Special packaging is prepared for festivals such as Chinese New Year, Hari Raya, Mother's Day, Mid-Autumn (Mooncake) Festival, Deepavali, and Christmas. The company prides itself on being the pioneer of cake redemption vouchers for weddings and baby first-month celebrations, relieving customers of having to send boxes of cakes personally to friends and relatives.

Bengawan Solo's distinctive brand starts with its charming and melodious name which was taken from a beautiful folk song about the longest river in Java, Indonesia. The song praised the wonder of nature and the history that the river carried. Enjoyed by both young and old, Bengawan Solo was immediately associated with natural, wholesome goodness. Selecting this name reflects the founder's philosophy of providing home-made quality cakes using only natural ingredients, a value that has been kept for over 26 years.

Traditions aside, one of the major reasons for Bengawan Solo's success lies in its ability to understand and respond to the changing needs of its customers. The retail outlets are fashioned like Western deli counters with its *kueh* neatly and attractively arranged for easy selection. Coconut-based *kueh* and fresh cream cakes are placed in refrigerated display shelves to maintain freshness. The outlets are conveniently located in housing estates, shopping centers, and business districts, and have extended opening hours to cater to working people. To Bengawan Solo's customers, a box of *kueh* represents a well-deserved tea break, a token of appreciation, or an enjoyable gathering with friends where everyone can enjoy its great taste together.

How does the company continue with its commitment to provide home-made quality products and yet meet the growing demands of its customers? The formula is its quality control, use of fresh natural ingredients, traditional cooking methods, and semi-automated processes. Just-in-time production and delivery is practiced for both the finished products and key raw materials in which the company pays a premium for locally produced eggs which are delivered daily, and coconuts freshly grated and pressed into juice only upon demand. Investment has been made in innovative food preparation equipment such as automated stirring and mixing, encrusting, revolving oven, and rotating steamer in order to maintain product quality and meet volume demand.

The founder supervises the production processes personally by visual examination and random tasting and enforces quality checks at every stage before it reaches the customer. Many of the *kueh* have a one-day shelf life due to the use of fresh ingredients with no preservatives added. Products unsold by the end of the day are returned to the factory for disposal while those with a longer shelf life are color-coded for First-In-First-Out inventory control as well as recall purposes. Customers are therefore confident that they are buying only the best quality products either for their own consumption or as gifts. The founder pledges that she has never and will never cut corners or sell products that are not fresh. That is the promise of the owner-entrepreneur who won the first Woman Entrepreneur of the Year Award from the Association of Small and Medium Enterprises (ASME) in Singapore in 1998.

In the years ahead, the company plans to focus its efforts on consolidating and building up its operations and image, strengthening its retail presence in Singapore, and exploring opportunities in new foreign markets. Its outlets at Singapore Changi Airport are strategically placed to give the brand an initial exposure to foreigners. As the company continues to grow both in sales and number of employees, the company is planning for a transition from a family-run business to a professionally managed corporation to facilitate the expansion locally and overseas. The main criterion for the company's expansion is that it must maintain the quality of all its products and ensure that they are of exactly the same standard as those made on the very first day of its existence. It strives to remain true to its roots of making fine traditional cakes and snacks for families and friends.

Bengawan Solo has successfully positioned itself as the convenient quality gift and souvenir shop of choice. Singapore is the place to shop and feast. To find treats and gifts that distinctly present the true flavors of Singapore, customers intuitively go to Bengawan Solo for perennial favorites, seasonal cakes, or celebratory specials. Content differentiation lies in its beautifully packed hand-made premium cakes, *kueh*, and cookies made from natural ingredients. Context differentiation is the convenience of ordering and collection of its freshly baked and perishable gifts through the use of vouchers and accessibility to its many well-located countrywide branches. The reinforcement from these differentiations strengthens Bengawan Solo's brand which is associated with quality, convenience, and the place for the perfect gift of good taste.

Bengawan Solo's strategic business triangle is based on local knowledge and in-depth understanding of local tastes and culture. Its product positioning of premium quality and convenient gift choices firmly differentiate the company from its competitors and creates a strongly entrenched brand name in Singapore.

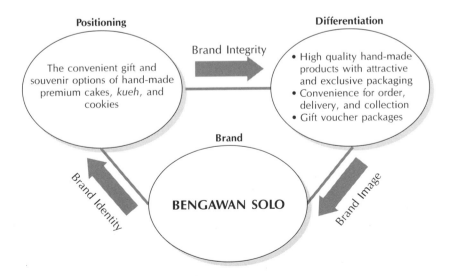

Figure 5.1   Positioning-differentiation-brand triangle of Bengawan Solo

Dji Sam Soe

Kretek or clove cigarette originated in Indonesia in the early 1880s. It was used for medicinal purposes as a way to deliver the eugenol in the cloves to the lungs of victims of asthma and chest pains. The cigarettes are made with a complex blend of tobacco, cloves, and special flavoring which gives a spicy aftertaste and pungent smell. The tradition and growth of *kretek* smoking were due mainly to its perceived therapeutic effect, health treatment, and odor-masking properties. There is some truth in this as eugenol extracts from cloves are used in perfumeries, flavorings, essential oils, antiseptics, and anesthetics.

In Indonesia, smoking is a tradition as well as a status symbol, especially for the men. The tobacco industry is a core contributor to the government's yearly revenue and one of the top five employers in the country. *Kretek* smoking is a social custom in Indonesia, much like the Western cigar gatherings of gentlemen's clubs. The best quality, premium *kretek* are handed out and enjoyed in prestigious and esteemed company of friends, business associates, and dignitaries. For many connoisseurs, Dji Sam Soe is to premium clove cigarettes what *kretek* is to Indonesia.

The century-old brand that has survived complete seizure during the Japanese invasion, a destructive factory fire, and four generations of family-run operations, was created by a Chinese immigrant named Liem Seeng Tee and his wife. They started a small-scale cigarette company called Sampoerna in 1913, making hand-rolled clove cigarettes which they dubbed Dji Sam Soe (meaning two, three, four in the Hokkien dialect). Although they tried making filtered cigarettes, Dji Sam Soe remains the most demanded and favored producer of *kretek* by all its customers.

The company was managed and operated by family members until 1963 when the production process was entrusted to external professionals while the founder's sons continued to control the business. The new generations of the clan were schooled overseas and possessed knowledge of international management. Combined with strong inborn business acumen, the Liem family employed new methods of increasing sales and marketing the Dji Sam Soe brand by creating a cost-effective and productive value chain. To support distribution of its products nationwide, a transportation and freight company was established in 1981. When a new factory was built in 1982, it was designed to house a laboratory to undertake research and tests to ensure adherence to international standards governing cigarette flavoring.

Through various expansions and acquisitions, the Sampoerna empire became one of the largest conglomerates in Indonesia with diversified businesses in banking, car manufacturing, food manufacturing, retail, and telecommunications. However, many of these ventures did not yield the expected results and the family decided to refocus on its core business of producing cigarettes, and broadened its cigarette distribution to other countries such as the Philippines, Malaysia, Vietnam, Myanmar, and Brazil. That turned out to be a wise move as the divestments helped Sampoerna to pull through the financial crisis in the late 1990s.

In 2000, the company recorded Rp10.03 trillion in net sales, an increase from the previous year. Total cigarette volume was up 2.4% and machine-made cigarettes reversed a two-year decline with a 7.4% increase. Volumes of Dji Sam Soe hand-rolled cigarettes reached new highs while the aggregate segment share fell to 37%. The same year, the company was the market leader in nine largest cities in Indonesia with its market share exceeding 30%.

The success of the brand was mainly due to clever marketing, quality products, and satisfying the emotional desires of its consumers. The general perception is that one is not a true smoker if he has not puffed a stick of Dji Sam Soe. With its distinctive packing, the brand spells out prestige and luxury, and creates a sense of accomplishment, status, and success. To the working class, smoking Dji Sam Soe is something they aim to achieve, like dining in a five-star restaurant or being in the company of high society.

According to a 2004 Ministry of Health report, 62.2% of Indonesian men smoked in 2001, compared to 1.3% of women. More than two-thirds of smokers started smoking before they turned 19. Tobacco has a long history in Indonesia and is rich with cultural symbolism and associations that existed before the advent of advertising. Dji Sam Soe used advertisements of its indigenous cigarettes to appeal to and reflect a fascinating concoction of unique Indonesian cultural values and desires. Sampoerna's 1996 annual report stated that "the relevance to the consumer of a brand's image and lifestyle will be the defining characteristic for success in the years to come" referring to its mass marketing to link lifestyle attributes to cigarette smoking.

Dji Sam Soe's "coming of age ritual" campaign reinforces the macho image that is shown in a typical commercial where a young man shoots his first boar; his father congratulates him on becoming a man and offers him his first stick of Dji Sam Soe. Besides TV commercials and billboard advertisements, the company is an active sponsor of jazz concerts and sports events such as the Copa Dji Sam Soe Indonesia, an annual football competition organized by the Indonesian Football Association, the world cycling meet Tour d'Indonesia, and the BMW Motorrad custom motorcycle display show.

Value creation and heart share are two winning objectives of the Dji Sam Soe brand. Every stick is hand-rolled with the best cloves and tobacco procured fresh from their sources through Sampoerna's networked supply chain. The hand-rolled cigarettes are individually wrapped in premium paper and packed in specially designed boxes. The company positions itself extremely high in consumers' emotional value through classy presentation of its products. The new super premium label, Magnum 234, presents a lush image of pure black on gold satin with bold taglines like "Unlock ultimate taste," "Black belt in *kretek*," and "The filter moment has come." In addition, the auspicious logo "234" which adds up to the lucky 9 is always featured in every cigarette and box. It invites anyone who smokes the Dji Sam Soe brand to share the company's good fortune.

The management of the close relationship between the company, its customers, and the public is a great testimony of commitment to its products and brands. In 2003, the House of Sampoerna museum opened in Indonesia's second city, Surabaya, to showcase the amazing Sampoerna history and the art of cigarette making. The museum is housed on the former premises of a Dutch-era orphanage that was once used as a theater as well as a venue where founding Indonesian president Sukarno gave numerous speeches. Now accessible to the public free of charge, it is a big attraction for university students and foreigners. Inside the beautifully restored building, the distinctive fragrance of cloves and tobacco hangs heavy in the air as female staff demonstrates how to paste, roll, and snip with machine-like efficiency to produce more than 300 sticks of *kretek* per hour. Along the halls, cabinets display everything from old printing plates for cigarette packs to the founder's first bamboo stall, his first bicycle, and a book titled *Smoking Is Good for You*.

To the local folks, the House of Sampoerna is a testimony of Indonesia's most successful companies achieved through hard work, good management, and strong family bonding. For the thousands of foreigners streaming through the door each year, it is a "must-see" tourist attraction in Surabaya, something akin to visiting wine museums in France.

In his book *Kretek: The Culture and Heritage of Indonesia's Clove Cigarettes*, the author Mark Hanusz charmingly sums up Indonesia's smoking culture thus: "Carried on the warm breezes of a sultry tropic night, the scent of *kretek*—Indonesia's indigenous clove cigarette—is the aromatic soul of a nation, the fragrant embodiment of all things Indonesian." This very soul of Indonesia has been kept much alive and remains as invigorating to the people as it was first hand-rolled by Dji Sam Soe's creator almost a hundred years ago.

Similar to Bengawan Solo, the positioning of Dji Sam Soe is self-reinforced in its customers' minds. If Coca-Cola is regarded as the real cola drink, Dji Sam Soe is perceived by Indonesians as the authentic clove cigarette that commands the ultimate smoking pleasure for true smokers.

The premium cigarette company is also backed by its strong content differentiation of superior tar and nicotine levels, and the use of the finest cloves and tobaccos. But that is not all. Context differentiation in its smoking ritual and the "fortune" myth are ways in which the company targets its customers' hearts. Indonesians are known for their rituals as well as myths. There is pride among

Indonesians when they smoke the Dji Sam Soe brand as it symbolizes high status and bravery.

The key to the success of Dji Sam Soe is its sensitivity to local socio-cultural behaviors such as rituals and myths, and the understanding of old smoking tradition. Only a local player like Dji Sam Soe can produce clove cigarettes that are able to specifically fulfill the Indonesian taste and evoke the desired emotions. Therefore, despite strong anti-smoking campaigns and increase in health consciousness, Dji Sam Soe continues to remain the most profitable clove cigarette brand in the world.

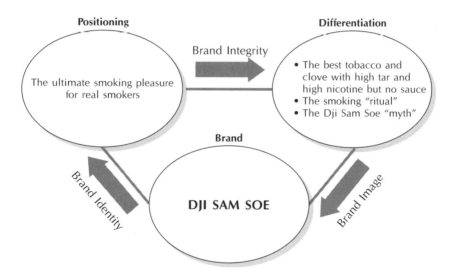

Figure 5.2   Positioning-differentiation-brand triangle of Dji Sam Soe

Goldilocks

When Filipinos need to give a thoughtful treat, they head for Goldilocks, the local bakeshop that has served fresh-from-the-oven *Pinoy* favorites since 1966. It is a brand that children have grown up with and adults can trust and approve. Started by two sisters, Clarita and Milagros, Goldilocks is representative of a true-blue home-grown success that Filipinos are proud of and find endearing. Just like Bengawan Solo in Singapore, Goldilocks' founders began with a passion for baking. They started by supplying chiffon cake slices to school canteens and making birthday cakes for mothers before they decided to turn their hobby into a commercial venture.

From a modest startup of ten employees, two display stands, and four tables cramped inside their first store, Goldilocks' small neighborhood goodie shop has turned into a billion-peso-earning food chain with more than 3,500 employees in the Philippines and the US. The founders' vision of producing high-quality but affordable products has guided the company throughout the years as it continues to grow and expand. Apart from its traditional rolls and chiffons, customers can now find a wide variety of intricate cakes, sweet delights, freshly baked breads, pies, tarts, native cakes, pastries, and *ensaymada* sweet breads from its bakeshop as well as full meal courses such as locally flavored pastas and *sarapinoy* meat dishes from its eat-in food shop.

The Goldilocks brand was designed for cake lovers to make an immediate connection of its yummy cakes and pastries with the favorite bedtime fairy tale loved by the masses. Based on the 2002 food and beverage consumer survey, Goldilocks boasts 100% total brand awareness and commands 71% "top-of-mind" awareness in the baking industry. Through its successful franchising program, the company is able to provide its customers with the same warm and inviting bakeshop environment and still keep the quality and value it has always been known for. With its assurance to customers that "There's bound to be a Goldilocks near you!" and "Once you step inside, you'll keep coming back for more" the company has steadily moved to become one of the top eight companies in the Philippines fast-food industry.

The Goldilocks franchising strategy started in 1991 as part of their expansion plan. Today, there are 82 stores in Metro Manila alone, 76 others spread around Luzon, 10 in Mindanao, 23 in Visayas, 17 in California, US and one in Vancouver, Canada. Each franchisee has the right to operate a specific Goldilocks store for a period of eight years and the use of the Goldilocks trade name and trademarks, proprietary products, store design, signage, and methods of operation in accordance with Goldilocks' established standards of quality, service, cleanliness, and customer service. To minimize the startup gestation period for new franchisees, Goldilocks provides a complete package including a delivery vehicle, operating equipment and utensils, collateral or surety bond, project management, store launching, point-of-sales system, and one-time training for one managing director, management team and crew members. Such measures are to ensure that every store that carries the Goldilocks name and products will meet the required high quality and standards.

On top of its carefully managed expansion of stores countrywide, the company continuously increases its spread of delectable goodies to meet the changing tastes and lifestyles of Filipinos. Healthy but tasty new products such as sugar-free *Mamon* sponge cake, are launched periodically to create a lively and innovative environment which customers can count on for good quality and exciting food whenever they visit Goldilocks stores. Many of its products, such as *Polvoron* milk candy and *Pik-a-Pop* caramel popcorn, are also available in hypermarkets and grocery stores.

When Globe Telecom launched its breakthrough mobile commerce service in 2005, Goldilocks swiftly tied up with the Philippines telecommunications giant to accept Globe G-CASH as a mode of payment for purchases of food at its stores. This serves the young mobile generation well and adds a "cool" appeal to its dine-in crowd. Customers can also engage Goldilocks Party Funfeast for parties and celebrations at its stores or off-site in offices or homes. Goldilocks is also the exclusive licensee of popular characters like Winnie the Pooh, Mickey Mouse, and Disney Princesses which are hits with children for theme parties.

Be it via *bitbit* (hand-carry) or *padala* (send), Filipinos give more than food—they give their warmth and care. "How thoughtful," Goldilocks' tagline, is shared by all Filipinos. From classic favorites, new goodies, delicious *ulam* toppings, and *merienda* snack dishes to party arrangements and *pasalubong* gift packages, Goldilocks continues to serve the local people using international standards and local *Pinoy* values.

Goldilocks is another typical local success as the bakeshop with international standards catering to Filipino tastes. Its wide varieties of original recipes and cuisines that exude the *Pinoy* appeal clearly differentiate the bakery from its competitors. Augmenting the existing product richness, the appreciation of home values, and sentiments has made Goldilocks one of the most accepted brands in the Philippines.

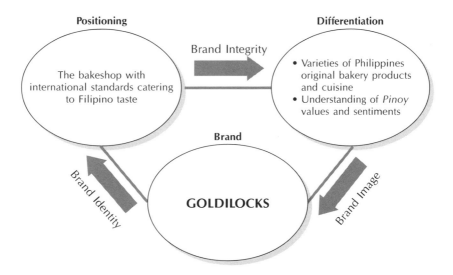

Figure 5.3   Positioning-differentiation-brand triangle of Goldilocks

MBF Cards

In 1987, a subsidiary of MBF Holdings Berhad, a Malaysian public listed investment and diversified business conglomerate, created news and broke new ground in the credit card industry with the first MasterCard International license in the country. MBF Cards made the bold move to introduce MasterCard credit card in a market that was already established by banks and rival card company Visa International. Armed with a high ambition and focused marketing, MBF Cards built a member base from scratch to more than 500,000 card members and acquired the largest merchant network in Malaysia.

The leading credit and charge card company in Malaysia, MBF Cards is also the first mono-line and non-bank to be awarded with a Visa license in Malaysia and the ASEAN region. Another first by MBF Cards was the launch of the first "contactless" Visa Wave IC-chip-based EMV (Europay Mastercard Visa) card in the world on April 27, 2004. This allows card users to pay for purchases without the need for traditional "swipe and sign" by simply waving the card at a close range of 4 cm from a payment reader. In February 2006, the company launched the first-in-the-world MBF 2006 FIFA World Cup OneSMART™ MasterCard PayPass™ contactless card.

How did a young financial services company thrive so well in a highly competitive and commoditized market? Usage of credit cards has grown significantly in the last 15 years and MBF's entry into this industry was indeed very timely. Yet the average annual growth of 20% means that more and bigger players are attracted to the lucrative business of issuing and acquiring cards. Investment in this business is extremely high due to the stringent security requirements and exposure to fraud. Normally a service that only banks are involved in, credit card business is linked to strong financial backing, reputation, and credibility.

The success of MBF Cards is due mainly to its corporate philosophy of "Enriching our card members' lives through practical innovations." Innovation was indeed the corporate culture from the start when the company pioneered a new concept and brand to the country. The MBF Cards brand focuses on niche marketing which makes the company the largest issuer of niche cards. It positions itself as a card issuer to market segments with different passions and needs by giving the "wow" effect with continued innovation to impact the lives of Malaysians.

Recognizing that the market is made up of communities with shared interests, MBF Cards introduces cards with varieties of privileges to suit the varied appetites of different card members. The MBF Xuan card is designed for the Chinese-language market where cardholders get updates on Chinese art and cultural activities, and discounts on selected restaurants and performances. The Lady card celebrates the modern woman and her indulgences with privileges for beauty care, fine dining, shopping, and travel services from participating stores. Besides great discounts and clever tie-ups with retail companies, MBF Cards prides itself on being the champion of diversity and a contributor to society and environment at the same time.

For those inclined toward ecology, health, personal education, and charitable causes, Gaia Visa was created. MBF Cards contributes 0.1% of Gaia Visa cardholders' spending to charitable and environmental causes. On top of that, a special newsletter containing local and global environmental news, charitable and environmental activities, voluntary work, and opportunities to interact with individuals of similar interests is sent to all "green" members. The same scheme of 0.1% contribution is also available for other cards, such as AIMST, Budimas, and MCA to help raise funds for the Asian Institute of Medicine, Science and Technology (AIMST), Budimas (Children) Charitable Foundation, and Universiti Tunku Abdul Rahman (UTAR), respectively. Cardholders are therefore always rewarded with a "feel good" sensation every time they use MBF cards. Such ingenious and benevolent approaches have won customer loyalty and public conviction.

The philosophy of "enriching lives" matters greatly especially when it comes to customer service and product features. MBF Cards has been proactive in investing in technology and research and development of revolutionary value-added products and services. The Clik 'n Serve online service was created to allow card members to manage their card transactions, such as reporting of lost or stolen cards and change of personal information from the comfort of their homes or offices 24 hours a day. The Clik 'n Shop online shopping mall serves customers who are too busy to visit physical stores to browse or shop. Clik 'n Advertise allows members to place commercials in the daily newspapers. As a leader in the payment industry, MBF Cards has developed a comprehensive and efficient payment system for its customers that is not found in other card providers. Clik 'n Pay is an online bill payment service for the settlement of utilities, telecommunications, education, summons, and insurance. Bill payments are also available via mobile phones in mBillPay.

While increased spending is excellent for the company, MBF Cards is also interested in introducing savvy spenders and shoppers to prudent financial management and planning through articles in their newsletters. Staffed by about 750 dedicated employees and supported by a network of 26 branches in Malaysia, the company constantly comes up with creative products and services and exciting campaigns. Most of all, MBF Cards knows how to pull the heartstrings of the Malaysian people in ways plain vanilla credit card providers cannot do.

MBF Cards has set an example in Malaysia for local players in niche markets. With its astute positioning, the card company targets specific needs of customers that bigger companies find difficult to fulfill. In addition, its wide range of niche cards for different market segments and its early adoption of leading-edge technologies have helped to promote the MBF Card brand and to identify it as Malaysia's largest and most innovative issuer of niche cards.

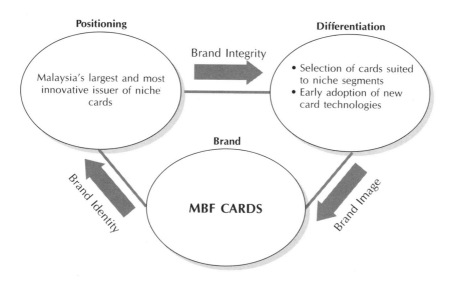

Figure 5.4   Positioning-differentiation-brand triangle of MBF Cards

Bangkok Hospital

Thailand, "the land of smiles," is best known around the world through two major musicals—Broadway's *The King and I* and London West End's *Chess*—and the 1984 hit song *One Night in Bangkok* written by ABBA. Though frowned upon by the Thais as uncomplimentary and biased depictions of their customs and culture, the shows and music gave the country immense publicity and attracted millions of curious tourists to this exotic destination for cheap entertainment, shopping, food, and other creature pleasures. Besides the draw of beautiful beaches, scenic countryside, and gentle hospitality, a new breed of travelers is flocking to the country for very different reasons—medical and health enhancement vacations.

According to Abacus International, medical tourism is becoming one of Asia's fastest growing industries, projected to be worth at least US$4 billion by 2012. The promise of low-cost, high-quality healthcare is attracting more than 1.3 million tourists a year to key locations such as Thailand where a medical tourist spends an average of US$362 a day, compared with the average traveler's spending of US$144. Bangkok Post 2004 Mid-Year Review states that healthcare costs in Thailand are 50% cheaper than in Singapore, three times cheaper than in Hong Kong, and five to ten times cheaper than in Europe and the US. A segment of the CBS investigative news program *60 Minutes* that aired in September 2005 featured Thailand as the leading medical tourism center where patients were given first-class service at third-world prices. For example, a hip replacement in the US could cost US$39,000 but only US$3,000 in Thailand. Reasons for the rise in medical tourism are the lack of health insurance, high costs of healthcare, and increasing needs of non-insurable procedures such as cosmetic surgeries and infertility treatments.

In the burgeoning medical industry, one hospital stands out as the best among the best in Thailand—Bangkok Hospital. Established in 1972 by a group of doctors and pharmacists, it started with five specialists and 30 full-time nurses to become the country's largest private hospital group with more than 400 full-time consultant physicians and 600 nurses. Its medical network expanded from the flagship hospital to 12 hospitals, 16 specialist centers, and 15 clinics in many provinces in its home country and eight other facilities in Cambodia, Vietnam, Myanmar, and Bangladesh.

The specialized centers come complete with the latest diagnostic and treatment methods and range from pediatrics to geriatrics, neurology to cardiology, and ophthalmology to treatments for sports-related injuries. In 2000 the Bangkok Heart Institute was the first in Thailand to offer off-pump surgery and minimally invasive cardiac surgery which reduces wound size and time requirement for the surgical procedures, resulting in faster recovery for the patient. For emergency coronary cases, a mobile Coronary Care Unit was introduced in 2003 to fill a critical gap in general ambulance service. The only unit of its kind in Thailand, it is staffed by an experienced coronary doctor and two nurses to treat chronic heart patients on their way to the hospital.

The Bangkok Neurological Gamma Center is the first and only hospital in Thailand that possesses the amazing gamma knife technology. This treatment of neurological diseases is a better and less risky alternative to conventional brain surgical treatment that exposes patients to many complications caused by infections and anesthetics. The center, being the only one in the country, is also an "open center" where any qualified physician from the government and the private sector can admit their patients who are in need of the gamma knife treatment.

Outpatient clinics are designed around the requirements of patients with different cultural and personal needs. These clinics are designed with unique facilities, such as the International Medical Services, Japanese Medical Services, and Arabic Medical Services. There are essentially four groups of clinics providing medical care. The Internal Medicine Clinic treats those suffering from acute and chronic ailments such as hypertension, diabetes, ulcers, and common infectious diseases. The Surgery Clinic provides day and minor surgeries for appendicitis, varicose vein, thyroid diseases, wounds, and other ailments. The Obstetrics and Gynecology Clinic provides full medical consultation and treatment for problems such as infertility, high-risk pregnancy, congenital abnormalities, and gynecologic cancer. The Special Clinic deals with psychiatry disorders such as depression, insomnia, and children's behavioral problems.

Continuous development and investment in the latest technology, medical expertise, and supporting facilities have contributed to the hospital's current status and reputation as one of the top medical institutions in Southeast Asia. Its vision statement is dedicated to maintaining the highest internationally accepted standards of medical practice by delivering quality patient care to each visitor in order to attain its paramount objective—"our patients' complete satisfaction."

Recently, the group invested US$150,000 in a videoconferencing system to link all its hospitals, clinics, and medical professionals around the country. The system helps to improve communications and allows the sharing of X-rays, magnetic resonance imaging, and other medical images with minimal loss of quality. The videoconferencing facility minimizes time for administrating treatment and discussing cases among the specialists and physicians in the different centers located around the country. With this, the group can operate its branches as a single entity and patients can count on a comprehensive attentive medical service.

The Thai government's aggressive drive for the country to be a regional healthcare hub has encouraged Bangkok Hospital to raise its bed capacity and look beyond serving the local market. In 2004 alone, the group treated 10,000 outpatients and 1,000 in-patients daily. Its latest addition, the Bangkok International Hospital, is staffed with an international team to provide people from different countries a comfortable and reassuring ambience to make their stay a pleasant one. Besides the hotel-style rooms and specially catered meals to suit every dietary requirement, patients can gain access to the hospital's 26-language translation service to assist them in making enquiries, and to explain medical conditions and give out instructions. In-patients are attended to promptly and professionally with careful consideration for their special cultural, personal, and religious needs. The welcome for international visitors starts with airport pickup, round-the-clock contact for medical assessments, advice on treatment options and doctors' appointments, liaison with embassies and international organizations, claims liaison with insurance companies, travel advice, and 24-hour medical evacuation and repatriation. On top of these, patients can select to have special Thai massages and grooming services in their own rooms, thereby easing the tension of undergoing a medical treatment.

Bangkok Hospital won two first prizes at the Asian Hospital Management Award 2002 presented by Options Information Company in cooperation with The International Hospital Federation, Johns Hopkins International, and The Private Hospital Association of Thailand; with special participation from The Summa Foundation, to support hospitals in the Asia-Pacific region for the delivery of affordable quality health services and products. The hospital has received various accreditations and awards for quality standards such as ISO 9002 and 9001, the Prime Minister's Export Award for Best Service Provider, accreditation by the Ministry of Public Health of Thailand, and Superbrands status by Superbrands International. It was the first private hospital in Thailand to receive the Board of Investment Promotion Privileges and it won first prize at the Hospital Management Asia Awards 2002 for the project of Integration of Quality Improvement by using the Standard Requirements of Hospital Accreditation and Brand Management.

Committed to providing medical services of the highest internationally accepted standards, the hospital employs the most appropriate and up-to-date practices and technology in all fields of medicine. In 2005, the hospital embarked on a rebranding strategy to renew its corporate image to reflect its business growth and leadership in Thailand's healthcare industry. A fresh logo was launched to differentiate and modernize the 33-year-old hospital icon and to give it a more international and inspiring appeal.

As a pioneer of medical care in Thailand, Bangkok Hospital has served both local and foreign communities with promptness and professionalism in world-class facilities at reasonable prices for over three decades, making it difficult for its closest competitors to follow its success.

Bangkok Hospital is positioned as the convenient and integrated healthcare solution. This positioning is possible because of its well-established infrastructure. As mentioned in the introduction of Part II, differentiation can be created from content, context, and infrastructure. The earlier four cases are companies that rely on content and context as their main differentiation. In the case of Bangkok Hospital, the network of hospitals and clinics with comprehensive integrated healthcare solutions is a fine example of infrastructure differentiation.

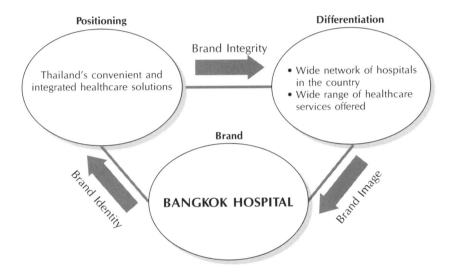

Figure 5.5   Positioning-differentiation-brand triangle of Bangkok Hospital

Number One Tonic Drink in Vietnam

The years of 1996, 1997, and 1998 are well remembered for the fierce competition between giant global brands, the explosion of fresh ideas for new products, and the amazing appearance of local brands in the refreshment drink market in Vietnam. Pepsi and Coca-Cola entered the Vietnamese market at the beginning of the 1990s with policies to extend joint ventures with state-owned companies, and managing their businesses through their share of contributed capital. A successful penetration strategy was followed by various tactics to secure a firm position in the Vietnam market. These corporations subsequently implemented a strategy to transform their businesses into 100% foreign-owned entities, made possible with the open-door policy of the Vietnamese government.

Opportunities for the Small Fry

The war between these two giants started in 1996. Both companies launched various activities through their advertising and promotional campaigns such as changing the packaging of their products, providing discounts to agents, slashing prices, dishing out promotional gifts, or increasing credits to agents. However, these strategies brought about huge losses for both brands from 1996 until 2000. The joint ventures stayed unprofitable through the years, and the local management reverted to foreign hands. The transformation of Pepsi and Coca-Cola into 100% foreign-owned companies became a reality.

The small and medium-sized companies operating in the refreshment business were the ones that suffered the most damage. They were continuously losing their market shares, their control of distribution channels, and their credit solvency. A number of companies merged and operated in smaller markets, while others became shareholding entities and strategically changed their businesses to different categories of products and market segments, following the old saying "Avoiding the elephant is not a shame." However, that situation also created new opportunities for other domestic businesses. While big corporations were fighting for market shares for their traditional products, local companies were entering the competition through the development of new products. A great number of drinks containing natural extracts such as soya, grapefruit, carrot, yogurt, and tea made their appearance, thus creating much variety for the refreshment market. The emergence of Number One tonic drink was the result of this creative process.

Number One is a brand of Tan Hiep Phat Company. In 2001, when the market of tonic drinks occupied only 0.67% of the total refreshment market, there were only three main brands—Red Bull, Rhino, and Lipovitan. All these products were marketed in cans and were distributed through agents who possessed coolers or refrigerators.

Red Bull and Lipovitan had their own factories in Vietnam, while Rhino was an imported product. At that time, those were the three biggest brands in Vietnam. Their advantages lay in their financial power and their ability to generate wide promotion through various communication media and hiring professional distributors to spread their products to every corner of the country. The main activities of those companies were still focused on selling and promoting.

Product Differentiation

Despite their financial power, experiences, and marketing knowledge, the big brands could not fulfill the demands of all market segments. According to research conducted in 2000, middle-class consumers were not able to afford a can of tonic drink at the price of 6,000 VND (40 US cents). Also, the majority of consumers experienced much inconvenience in the consumption of tonic drinks as they did not have in-house refrigerators. So when the need arose, they had to go to shops to buy and consume the drinks. One important factor was that tonic drink taken with ice was not as good as when it was chilled.

On the consumption psychology, researches showed that the majority of consumers understood that "tonic drink" was the product that brought comfort, enhanced body and spiritual function, relieved stress, and helped them work better. These were important perceptions that had been exploited by big brands in the market penetration strategies, pricing, and distribution of their products.

For Number One, these perceptions were the foundation to boldly invest in this market. Tan Hiep Phat decided to invest in a factory to produce bottled tonic drink in Vietnam. During the first phase, they manufactured 300-ml bottles and sold them at low prices to make them affordable to the majority of local consumers. Convenience and particularly the fact that this drink could be taken with ice—without losing its good taste—were the new advantages. An important factor is that consumers were used to drinking from a bottle. Number One was the only bottled tonic drink in the market at that time, with a selling price equivalent to a bottle of Coke or Pepsi at 2,500 VND (18 US cents).

Focused on Consumers' Convenience

Product differentiation was a significant factor contributing to the success of Number One. Another significant factor was the consumption habit of consumers. Local consumers drank tonic drinks at street refreshment stalls or small coffee shops. They seldom consumed it at home. Market research showed that 15% of consumers in five cities brought home tonic drinks once a week. Hence, 85% had their tonic drinks at coffee shops. This was mostly due to the fact that many did not own a refrigerator, and also because they preferred to take their drinks with ice.

Being able to consume tonic drinks at low prices was "hot" during the year 2001. People with average incomes formed the majority of tonic drinkers. As it was the first bottled tonic drink in Vietnam, consumers could enjoy it anywhere. This was the main reason that helped Number One quickly capture customers and transform the competitive landscape in the refreshment market in Vietnam at that time.

Building Brand

The three main elements that brought success to the branding strategy of Number One were product, distribution, and effective communication. Equipment and production technology were imported from Europe to set up a manufacturing process that was modern, safe, and hygienic. These images were well communicated on various TV channels and created a strong, positive impact on consumers nationwide.

Within four months of its launch, Number One tonic drink captured 30% market share. Total distribution channels included 300,000 outlets with more than 200 distributors in all the 64 provinces and cities. Business was so good that Number One did not have enough supply to satisfy the demand during festivities such as the Lunar New Year.

Pepsi and Coca-Cola lost their market shares in a number of market sectors, and they forced their exclusive distributors not to carry and distribute products for Number One. But a dramatic event happened: many new distributors not beholden to Pepsi or Coca-Cola appeared in big cities. They transformed the whole distribution system and the distribution policies of competitors.

One factor that had contributed to the success of Number One was the very effective advertising campaign carried out by THP Group marketing division and its agency, the then Saatchi & Saatchi Vietnam. The communication was quite simple: during one whole month, a five-second teaser was aired on the two main TV channels in Vietnam with only one message: "Bottled tonic drink has appeared in Vietnam." This campaign created a big impact among the audience. At that time, market research showed that 60% of consumers had tried and 30% had later become regular consumers of Number One. Along with the strong advertising message were posters pasted on the walls of shops that sold Number One. Promotional items such as ice boxes, uniforms, flag-lines, glass containers, and glasses were provided to support sales in the whole country.

Since 2002, Number One has also focused on its public communication campaign. It officially sponsored the bicycle race and the HCMC TV Cup, a race where participants ran from Ho Chi Minh City to the capital Hanoi and back. The last day of the race ended right on April 30 which marked the commemoration day of Vietnam's reunification. This is the most prestigious race in Vietnam and the sponsorship not only garnered daily news coverage of the race, but also bore testimony to the credibility and strength of a local brand. In 2005, all above- and below-the-line activities ceased completely. Number One is now concentrating on being the main sponsor of the Vietnam Football Cup (V-League) with an amount of 10 billion VND (US$650,000). This is the biggest football competition in Vietnam.

Besides that, Number One is currently sponsoring the Social Activities Center of the HCMC Youth Branch to create a web site called "Live beautifully" for more than 200 secondary and preparatory schools and universities nationwide. The aim of the web site is to disseminate knowledge, highlight real-life situations about the behavior, study, and work of young people, and guide them to better goals in their lives.

Conclusion

The current success of Number One has prepared them for product extension: Number One in can, Number One Soda, Number One Soya. These are growing on the foundation of a strong main brand.

After only four years, the Number One line of products has managed to occupy more than 65% of the tonic bottled drink market, with brand recognition amounting to 80%, and taking up more than 20% of the bottled refreshment drink market. This is an amazing success.

The success of Number One is due to the correct assessment of the situation and demand of the market, bold investments, and implementations of appropriate strategies in the manufacturing of quality products, strong distribution channels, and an effective branding strategy. This lesson is a valuable experience for small and medium-sized enterprises which have to compete in a big arena. Number One's success can be summarized as follows:

1. The differentiation is that it is the first bottled tonic drink in Vietnam.

2. Low selling price, affordable to all economic classes in a country that has a population of more than 80 million people.

3. A surprise element. The launch of a new product in the bottled tonic category is a big challenge for local manufacturers which have weak financial and technological power. This is a product of a newly established company, so big competitors did not pay much attention and did not have offensive schemes in time until Number One had the upper hand.

4. Appropriate positioning through the creation of convenience in usage. The ability to make the product easily is a winner. In a country where 65% of the population are young people, and 80% of the population depend on an agricultural economy, the marketing of a low-priced tonic drink that is safe and hygienic is a bright marketing idea.

5. Having an effective brand-building strategy. It was the first company in Vietnam to take the initiative to hire the services of multinational advertising agencies to carry out advertising campaigns in a professional way.

6. Well-exploited public relations activities such as sponsored football events and sponsored charity and social activities. These are "must-do" activities for companies operating in the fast-moving consumer goods industry and wishing to succeed in Vietnam.

7. With an invested capital of 2 million VND since the launch of its products, Number One has become the leading bottled tonic drink in Vietnam with an annual output of about 7 million cases per year.

8. Number One has been able to compete in a big market on its own terms. Its business strategy transformed the market and secured a firm position for itself.

9. Another important factor is the strong business spirit of the founder of the THP group. In the context of an unbalanced competitive situation where the notion of the brand was still new in Vietnam, innovative thinking and execution and his untiring efforts were elements that contributed to making Number One a familiar brand for the Vietnamese consumers.

Number One is an example of a company that has successfully positioned itself as a pioneer brand. Declared as the first bottled tonic drink in Vietnam, Number One has been made available to everyone due to its widespread distribution and price affordability. Its bottling technology adds to its differentiation from other tonic drinks and increases customer perception of its brand.

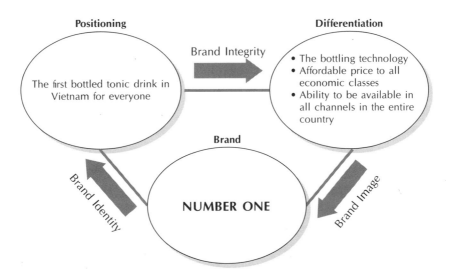

Figure 5.6   Positioning-differentiation-brand triangle of Number One

Lessons Learned

The main thing that we can learn from local champions is that they fully understand the desires and anxieties of their local customers. Bengawan Solo, Dji Sam Soe, Goldilocks, and Number One perform well simply because they are able to address the needs of the local markets better than any foreign companies.

Another lesson is that local champions usually take the niche markets to flank the bigger players which are mostly multinationals. The case of MBF Cards exemplifies this. Large corporations are relatively more reluctant to target niche markets as they find the small customer base difficult to manage and justify in terms of product customizations.

Compared to less flexible business giants that provide standardized products and services to worldwide markets, local champions can be as intimate as possible with their customers. This is their biggest advantage. All the cases describe this. Although the companies discussed here are relatively big in their respective countries, they are small compared to the multinationals. This often spurs the local companies on to try harder to gain the respect and loyalty from their customers.

chapter 6

Learn from the Locals Going ASEAN

Growth is the oxygen of business, the key to a business's life or death.
Growing enterprises thrive; shrinking companies vanish.

Michael Treacy

Expansion is a natural progression of growth. When the home market becomes saturated and highly competitive, progressive companies must look for new markets and customers overseas. In the previous chapter, we discussed how local champions continue to do well in their niche markets at home, even in the presence of global competitors. The effects of globalization and technological advances may one day force these companies to seek new markets as well in order to survive.

For ASEAN companies planning to venture overseas, the best place to start is in ASEAN itself. Besides the close proximity and advantageous trading conditions, the region offers a huge consumer market of 540 million people. Local companies that have successfully established themselves overseas have all started by branching into the neighboring countries first before expanding internationally. To learn from their experiences, we look at five of these: Extra Joss from Indonesia, Royal Selangor from Malaysia, San Miguel from the Philippines, Eu Yan Sang from Singapore, and Black Canyon from Thailand. These companies are household names in their own countries and leaders in their own industries. Through careful planning, product focus, and consistent quality and value, the companies are able to win the trust and loyalty of consumers in all the new markets that they expand into. Such is the strength of credible branding.

Extra Joss

For centuries, Indonesians have relied on traditional Javanese herbal medicines or *jamu* for relieving stress, boosting stamina, and increasing alertness. Making *jamu* is a lengthy process and normally done at home. Commercial *jamu* started as a cottage industry where the reddish-brown or golden colored liquid was peddled door to door by women offering a quick pick-me-up in a bottle for tired housewives, farmers, and factory workers.

In recent times demand for *jamu* and new stimulants has increased as people sought ways to help overcome daily health problems arising from political, social, and economic crises. In the context of prevalent changing conditions and lifestyles, different sorts of supplements, tonics, and energy drinks have emerged from large drug or food manufacturers in the country. One of the most successful is Extra Joss produced by pharmaceutical giant Bintang Toedjoe. Since its first appearance in 1994, Extra Joss has become Indonesia's hottest new product with sales exceeding all expectations and an impressive market share of 60%. In its introductory year, total sales amounted to Rp 65 million per month. At the end of 2001, the figure skyrocketed to Rp 45 billion per month.

Extra Joss energy pack comes in small sachets of instant powder or a tablet form and costs much less than bottled energy drinks. Targeted at the low-income drinkers, the company removed the high cost of bottling and canning to offer the product at an affordable price. The cheap energy source is distributed nationwide and is readily available in all retail outlets from small convenience roadside stalls to modern hypermarkets. To differentiate itself from its bottled competitors, Extra Joss positioned the core value in its contents and not the bottle with the official tagline in Bahasa Indonesia, *"Ini Biangnya Buat Apa Beli Botolnya."* ("Why buy the bottle?") A unique selling point, the tactic successfully associated the brand with the "biang" (why) generation and a special GenBi zone was created to promote ideas and activities for the energetic, young, inquisitive, innovative, dynamic, and outgoing.

The no-fuss energy drink that comes in one flavor of core concentrate was promoted by well-known personalities from musicians to sportsmen like Italian football star Alessandro del Piero who endorsed the drink with the strong message "Don't give up, drink Extra Joss." Extensive advertisements and sponsorships of major public events were part of the company's strategy to reach out to the masses. After the Sydney 2000 Olympic Games, the company presented Rp 1 billion bonus to every Indonesian gold medal winner. Extra Joss was also the official sponsor for the live coverage of World Cup 2002 on RCTI (a private Indonesian television station). During Manchester United's Far East Asia 2005 tour, a TV commercial featured Christiano Ronaldo discovering the secret to incredible physical strength and stamina of the Indonesians, which was the amazing drink Extra Joss.

Although it may seem extravagant, the company's promotional and publicity campaigns aim to touch the hearts of millions of Indonesian consumers by enticing them to be part of the "in" group through support of the powerful drink. Advertisements are strategically used to communicate the brand through the people's favorite activities such as music, soccer, and boxing. While effective branding plays an important role in a product's success, Extra Joss is mostly sought after because it delivers what it promises. The main consumers are active adults below 35 years old who are always perceived to have the zest for life or have physically demanding jobs. As the consumer pattern changed and included the working class, the company launched a ready-to-drink version in a snazzy can to target the middle- and high-income market segment that will pay more for added convenience.

From its inception to 2002, Extra Joss was distributed exclusively by one of the most reputable and largest distribution chains in the country at that time. This arrangement allowed the company to concentrate on its production and brand building in Indonesia and to explore new markets in the region. Following its success in its home country and armed with several prestigious awards for best brand, total customer satisfaction, national consumer quality, and Asia-Pacific excellence, Bintang Toedjoe was ready to market Extra Joss overseas.

The company has already established a branch in the Philippines and has plans to expand to other ASEAN countries such as Malaysia and Vietnam. These have similar demographics and lifestyles as Indonesia and are identified as ideal consumer markets for the energy drink. Extra Joss has also found its way to retail shops in countries such as Singapore although the brand does not yet have an official representative. This is due to demand by Indonesians working overseas who yearn for the extra "oomph" and vigor which they can get at home.

Extra Joss' powerful core positioning as the essence of an energetic core generation has built up its strong brand personality of a young, healthy, full-of-energy, yet affordable product.

As the product expands to neighboring countries like the Philippines and Malaysia, the company's retail distribution experience plays an important part in reaching out to its customers and helps to build its brand overseas. Its strategic business triangle applies to other ASEAN countries as well with the same characteristic of dominant young generation markets. Extra Joss is poised to continue its growth overseas.

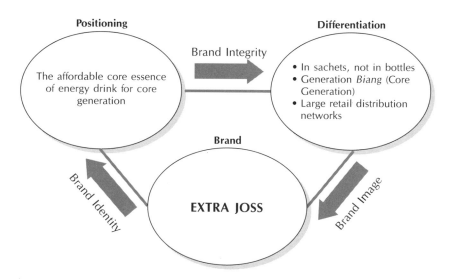

Figure 6.1   Positioning-differentiation-brand triangle of Extra Joss

Royal Selangor

In the world of pewter, Royal Selangor is as Malaysian a brand as champagne is French. Started in 1885 at a time when Malaysia was the largest tin producer in the world, the pewter company used the tin alloy to make handcrafted objects such as joss sticks holders and incense burners for ceremonial use on altars of Chinese homes and temples. With the arrival of British colonials, the company expanded its production to tankards, ashtrays, and English tea sets for local orders and export to the UK.

The 19th century craftsmanship arising from the little shop Ngeok Foh (Jade Peace) started by Chinese immigrant Yong Koon, was destined not just to make humble candlesticks and utensils but to produce exquisite pewter ornaments fit for a king. The company's name changed first to Selangor Pewter and later to Royal Selangor to reflect the royal endorsement from His Royal Highness, The Sultan of Selangor. With more than 500 skilled craftsmen in its factory in Kuala Lumpur, Royal Selangor produces over a thousand designs of tableware, desk accessories, photo frames, and gifts that are sold worldwide. Besides household items, Royal Selangor produces plaques, trophies, and medals which are well sought after by local and international corporate customers and sports organizations. These creations are for prestigious events such as the Formula One Malaysian Grand Prix and Sydney 2000 Olympics.

From the 1970s, the company began exporting its wares, first to Singapore, Hong Kong, and Australia, next to Europe, and then later to Japan. Today, it exports to over 20 countries and works with distribution agents to retail its products to some 8,000 independent jewelers, gift shops, and leading department stores such as Harrods of London, Mitsukoshi of Japan, and Myers and David Jones of Australia. Branches with warehousing facilities and wholly owned retail outlets in major shopping streets and malls have been established in Australia, Canada, China, Hong Kong, Indonesia, Japan, New Zealand, the Philippines, Singapore, Thailand, United Arab Emirates, the UK, and the US. Its flagship store at Suria KLCC (Kuala Lumpur Convention Center) offers a chic and comfortable ambience for admiring and selecting from the wide range of intricately designed yet amazingly functional pewter works of art.

Royal Selangor pewter adheres to international standards in its manufacturing process. The pewter is made mainly from tin with small proportions of copper and antimony as a strengthening agent. The soft, malleable nature of pewter allows designers to express individuality, beauty, and creativity in their work. The company's commitment to high quality, innovative designs, and outstanding craftsmanship has earned for itself many international awards for design excellence and custom-manufacturing facilities. In 2002, its Wine Celebration funnel won the grand slam of design competition by bagging three international awards—Germany's Red Dot, America's IDEA2002, and Japan's Good Design. In recent years, Royal Selangor has commissioned and collaborated with internationally known designers such as British Nick Munro and Danish Erik Magnussen to produce contemporary signature collections to cater to the changing tastes and sophistication of its customers. In 1996, the Victoria and Albert Museum in London worked with Royal Selangor to produce the romantic William Morris Wine Accessories collection which won the UK Gift of the Year award in 1997.

The forward-thinking company has also diversified into the design, manufacture, and marketing of precious jewelry and "925" hallmarked sterling silver under the names of Selberan and Comyns. In line with its debut into fashion, wearable pewter is grabbing the attention of the younger generation. Parents and older adults have taken to collecting designer accessories, good luck charms, and cute little keepsakes, all of which are promoted using the company's catchy tagline "Pewter has a new attitude." Stylish pewter designs have also found their way around the necks and stems of elegant crystal wine decanters and glasses. In 2006, the company announced that it will expand its business portfolio and product offerings into interior architecture. This move is not surprising, as Royal Selangor and an Australian company have jointly developed metalesce, a technique that fuses a coat of metal onto substrate material such as tile, wood, or plaster. This innovation will enable pewter and other metal derivatives to produce large feature walls, furniture, fittings, signage, and sculptures.

Royal Selangor has proudly and creatively presented its wonderful pewter ware as Malaysia's Gift to the World. Its service is impeccable and the company makes every effort to ensure a pleasant shopping experience for customers buying gifts for themselves or others. In addition to physical shops, an online store is created to enable customers to shop at Royal Selangor anytime, anywhere in the world. The visitor center in Kuala Lumpur, where visitors are treated to interactive exhibits, is a fascinating place to spend a day. Factory tours highlight the elaborate pewter-making and handcrafting processes and the intricate handwork that goes into the making of Selberan's fine jewelry. The "School of Hard Knocks" is an entertaining hour-long workshop where for a small fee, participants are taught to create their own pewter dish using traditional tools and methods.

The world's most innovative pewter craft company with its long tradition of superior quality where the majority of its pewter products are still hand-cast today continues to be the gracious gift giver. The true "touchmark," the signature of the company handed down from one generation to another, is manifested in Royal Selangor's unyielding and uncompromising efforts to make each and every pewter piece as aesthetic and as purposeful as possible for the homes, offices, and showcases of people who love the finer things in life.

Royal Selangor is another example of a local brand that has successfully expanded to other countries. Its positioning as the world's most innovative pewter crafter has made the brand famous around the globe. It is innovation that ensured this company's survival for more than a century with generations of highly skilled craftsmen producing a wide range of creative yet practical pewter ware. Its extensive distribution network allows Royal Selangor to be sold in North America, Europe, Australia, and New Zealand, as well as major Asian countries such as China and Japan, and ASEAN countries such as Singapore, Thailand, Indonesia, and the Philippines.

Figure 6.2   Positioning-differentiation-brand triangle of Royal Selangor

San Miguel

San Miguel Beer was started by Spaniard Don Enrique Maria Barretto de Ycaza in 1890 as *La Fabrica de Cerveza de San Miguel,* the first official brewery in Spanish-occupied Philippines and the whole of Southeast Asia. In 1913, La Fabrica became a corporation and began exporting beer from its Manila headquarters to Guam, Hong Kong, and Shanghai. After World War II, the beer pioneer built a brewery in Hong Kong in 1948, the first local brewer in the crown colony. Today, the San Miguel Beer Division (SMBD) has the capacity to produce 325 million cases of 320-ml bottles and is one of the largest selling beers and among the top 20 beer brands in the world.

From the original *cerveza* (beer in Spanish) that first rolled off the bottling line, San Miguel Corporation has since diversified to produce a wide range of beverages and food products which are consumed locally as well as exported to major markets around the world. Employing over 26,000 people in more than 100 facilities in the Philippines, Vietnam, Indonesia, Thailand, China, and Australia,

San Miguel Corporation is one of Asia's largest public-listed food, beverage, and packaging company.

San Miguel's cash cow and flagship product is still its trademark beers which command 90% of the Philippines market. Though internationally known, San Miguel is deeply entrenched in the Philippines with its City of Manila *escudo* (shield) logo and its pervasive presence from high-end restaurants and pubs to the local neighborhood stores. At town fiestas and big celebrations, cases of San Miguel beer are always available to make sure everyone has a good time. One of the popular San Miguel slogans *"Kahit Kailan, Kaibigan"* (always make time for friends) reflects the true traits of the Filipinos who treasure friendship, camaraderie, and *pakikisama* (cooperation). Filipinos down 1.2 billion liters of beer a year or roughly 15 liters per person. Beer alone accounts for 75% of the corporation's profits and over 80% of sales come from the Philippines. In 2004, sales volume reached an all-time high of 174 million cases.

Due to rising costs such as "sin" taxes and political and economic changes, sales margins in the Philippines have been sliding slowly. This does not mean that the corporation is not doing well. On the contrary, the 118-year-old company that has become so dominant at home with its 90% majority control over the beer market, 87% of soft drinks, 60% of processed meat, and 40% of the poultry consumed in the country, aims to achieve even more. In recent years, the seasoned international player embarked on an aggressive expansion program by tapping into its extensive overseas networks and experience in the overseas markets.

In January 2006, "San Miguel on the Move" was published to communicate the strategic direction and changes designed to make the corporation bigger and better. The entire exercise of consolidation and expansion is to increase competitiveness and build synergies in all business units and facilities across the Asia Pacific by reducing the cost of operations. San Miguel wants to be seriously regarded as a regional company which happens to have operations in the Philippines. It will continue to develop its line of products with universal brands as well as locally originated labels. With combined size, depth of portfolio, breadth of operations, and market reach, San Miguel's regionalization efforts will present opportunities outside, yet preserve the revenue stream from inside. At the same time, the company will increase its resistance against negative swings affecting business performance and financial health. This is hoped to be San Miguel's natural hedge.

"The leaps and bounds that are needed to achieve our vision can only come from acquisitions and regional expansion," San Miguel President Ramon S. Ang told *BusinessWeek*. Between 2003 and 2005 alone, San Miguel bought five companies in four nearby countries and boosted 2004 international sales to 13% of total revenues, from 10% in 2003.[1] Now San Miguel wants to get into more developed markets such as Australia and New Zealand and into emerging markets like India. Though many of the acquisitions are intended to diversify San Miguel's product and brand portfolio in its transformation from a Filipino beer manufacturer to regional food and beverage conglomerate, the beer sector remains its core business.

In Thailand San Miguel paid over US$100 million for Thai Amarit which includes a 21.75-hectare site with a fully equipped brewery with the capacity to produce one million hectoliters of beer yearly, and a 2.4-hectare property strategically located at the Bang Po area which comes with port facility and access to the Bangkok's Chao Phraya River. In Indonesia, the corporation acquired a multiproduct beverage factory located 25 kilometers from Jakarta in the Bekasi province which will complement the San Miguel's Anker Bir beer business in Indonesia, the second largest-selling beer in the country.

San Miguel's partnerships with major international companies have given the corporation access to the latest technologies and skills, and a local network of distributors and retailers. The equity investment of Japanese leading brewery, Kirin Brewery Company, in San Miguel has further enhanced San Miguel's competitive position in Asia, a region in which it is already well placed. San Miguel's Australian brewer, J. Boag & Son, is a leader in the fast-growing premium beer segment with James Boag Premium lager and other Boag's label beers.

San Miguel's shining star is in China where the corporation already has a clear lead over other foreign brands by having been

---

[1] Heinz Bulos, "San Miguel's Buying Binge," *BusinessWeek*, April 25, 2005.

in Hong Kong for almost a century, with a 24% share in the beer market. In 1994, the corporation acquired a Guandong brewery and inaugurated it as San Miguel Shunde Brewery. The Chinese brands Dragon and Valor have since become the most popular beers in the wealthy southern part of China. In North China beer making started in 1996 with San Miguel's purchase of the former Bada Baoding Brewery. In 2001 San Miguel's Blue Star beer was declared Baoding's Official Beer, as it was the bestselling beer in Baoding. A major factor contributing to Blue Star's continuing gains is the company's efforts to boost sales and sustain brand awareness and patronage, including participation in the annual Baoding Beer Festival. This annual event is China's "Oktoberfest," drawing the crowds from nearby densely populated Tianjin, Shijiazhuang, and China's capital, Beijing.

With over 30 beer labels to suit different tastes and local drinking habits, San Miguel has been successful in connecting with its consumers as the beer of choice that can be enjoyed regardless of location—along a hot, dusty Filipino street, on a weekend drinking binge Down Under, or in a pub in a freezing Chinese winter. "Making everyday life a celebration" is San Miguel's core purpose and statement to capture the corporation's enduring commitment to make its products, brands, and services so much a part of the consumer's everyday life.

San Miguel is one of the Philippines' best known export brands. Being the first brewery in ASEAN, it is the region's most famous beer. Long-time drinkers will probably profess that it is one of the best beers in the world. Its positioning as the unofficial national beer of the Philippines with excellent quality is reinforced in the minds of Filipinos who consider it as the first homemade beer in the country.

Because of its world-class quality brewing and large distribution networks, San Miguel's expansion to other countries has proved positive for the brand. With production in major ASEAN bases such as Thailand, Indonesia, and Vietnam, San Miguel will be more easily available across the region. The high availability in neighboring countries as well as in the home market is the key for consumer goods such as San Miguel to succeed.

Figure 6.3   Positioning-differentiation-brand triangle of San Miguel

Eu Yan Sang

Every Chinese community in the world will have at least a specialist store filled with jars and drawers of natural herbs and medicinal organs clearly labeled with names and grades of the contents. The *sinseh*, who is a trained physician or herbalist, will always be available to give advice on the best treatments and prescriptions for all kinds of ailments from flu to anemia, as well as health enhancements for having flawless complexion or balancing *yin-yang* in the body. The practice of diagnosing and treating ailments using the oriental philosophical concepts of *yin-yang*, the five elements, and the human body meridian system is referred to as traditional Chinese medicine (TCM). This traditional medical practice, which originated in China, has developed over the course of several thousand years and is commonly found in Japan, Korea, Tibet, Mongolia, and countries with ethnic Chinese settlements.

In Singapore, a name that is synonymous with TCM is Eu Yan Sang. Trusted by generations for over 126 years, the company was started by a Chinese immigrant, Eu Kong, in 1879 as Yan Sang Medical

Shop in Gopeng, a small mining town in Malaysia. The shop was set up to dispense TCM and herbs to improve health and as alternative treatments of sickness, physical fatigue, and pain for fellow immigrants who had fallen prey to opium addiction as an escape from the harsh conditions in the tin mines and plantations.

In Chinese, "Yan Sang" means caring for mankind and the benevolent Eu began a legacy that was dedicated to promoting responsible living through proper care and nourishment, and effective diagnosis and treatment of physical suffering with natural healing methods.

Today, Eu Yan Sang manufactures and markets over 1,000 types of fine-quality Chinese herbal cures and 250 proprietary medicines and health foods under its brand name. The consumer healthcare group has its own distribution network of more than 90 retail outlets in Hong Kong, Malaysia, Singapore, and the US. These outlets offer the full range of herbal supplements and medicines. In addition, the company operates a chain of 12 TCM clinics in Singapore and Malaysia, and six integrative medicine centers (IMCs) in Singapore and Australia that engage Western-trained doctors as well as TCM practitioners to attend to the needs of patients. Eu Yan Sang products such as *Bak Foong* pill, *Bo Ying* compound, and herbal candies are available in over 6,000 drugstores, pharmacies, medical halls, hospitals, supermarkets, health centers, and convenience stores worldwide.

Retail turnover grew by 21% in 2005 to S$108.9 million due to higher sales of its proprietary medicines, health foods, and herbs. Wholesale turnover rose 16% to S$34.3 million due to the increased demand of TCM herbs from hospitals in Hong Kong and China, and market growth in Australia and the US. The top five products are bottled bird's nest health supplement, *Bak Foong* female enhancement pill, *Bo Ying* infant remedy compound, *Lingzhi* immunity enhancement, and *Hou Ning* cough and phlegm cure. Through extensive research, new products are continuously introduced to health-conscious consumers who have benefited from Eu Yan Sang's prescriptions and have stayed loyal to its brand.[2]

---

[2] Eu Yan Sang Annual Report 2005.

Already a leading household name with Chinatown's main street Eu Tong Seng named after the founder's son, Eu Yan Sang is not one to rest on its laurels. In 1999, the company underwent a rebranding exercise with the launch of a new logo, store upgrading, and redesigned product packaging. The more contemporary image aims to revitalize the traditional practice of TCM to cater to the new generation of consumers who are mostly English-educated, busy, and used to Western-style shopping and consultation. Stores are designed to be more user-friendly and invite customers to browse and study the products and health tips—a far cry from the bitterly pungent apothecaries normally associated with TCM. The outstanding designs of its stores earned the Asia Pacific Interior Design Award in 1998 and 2003 and the rebranding program clinched the Design for Asia Award—Distinguished Designs from China on Total Branding Solutions by the Hong Kong Design Center in 2003.

The modernization of Eu Yan Sang is linked to its vision to be a global consumer healthcare company with a focus on TCM and integrative healthcare. It leads the way in how TCM will be presented and practiced in the future. Besides the physical changes in its stores and packaging, the rebranding involves the reorganization of the clinics. Eu Yan Sang's clinics are differentiated by "general practitioner" (GP) clinics and "specialist" clinics. The GP clinics offer strictly TCM treatments while the specialist clinics use both traditional Chinese and complementary Western practices to diagnose and treat patients. According to the Group Chief Executive, Mr. Richard Eu, the strategy will provide consultative services to meet the changing needs of consumers with an integrated East-West approach that will transform the delivery of medical services worldwide, thus giving consumers the best of both worlds. As the landscape of medicine is changing, conventional medicines and natural medicines like TCM can no longer be seen as mutually exclusive and opposing approaches to health management. With the new direction, Eu Yan Sang aims to be the preeminent brand in all aspects of TCM.

Caring for mankind is what the company does best. In 2003, Eu Yan Sang committed to using its expertise and resources to help Hong Kong fight SARS by donating anti-viral TCM products to frontline health workers in hospitals and charitable organizations. The company further collaborated with the Hong Kong Baptist University to publish *An Illustrated Chinese Materia Medica in Hong Kong*, the first of its kind to describe the origins, properties, and efficacies of 500 commonly used Chinese herbs and natural medicines complete with photographs and microscopic images. The joint project represented a two-year research effort to establish an industry platform on standardization and to advance modernization of the TCM sector.

Eu Yan Sang believes its competitive strengths are in its brand name and 126-year history and recognition in its key markets in Hong Kong, Singapore, and Malaysia. The company's scientific approach to offering quality herbs and Chinese proprietary medicines has served generations of customers in Asia and buillt invaluable goodwill with over 50,000 VIP customers and approximately 3,000 loyal customers who make purchases at its retail outlets daily. Most importantly, Eu Yan Sang has accumulated a wealth of knowledge in TCM products and experienced personnel who have served the company for more than 20 years each. Eu Yan Sang's rich heritage and a noble family tradition enable the company to stay true to its values of humanity, leadership, quality, and progress.

Eu Yan Sang's positioning as the branded TCM with extensive experiences in traditional Chinese herbs and medicine, works to differentiate it from other TCM companies in product quality and retail presence. Modern marketing helps to profile the 120-year-old brand effectively to the newer generations as a contemporary healthcare label with deep traditional roots. Although its presence in ASEAN is only in Singapore and Malaysia, the large number of outlets in the two countries makes the brand recognized across the region. Similar to Extra Joss and San Miguel, its widely accepted strategic business triangle enables well-organized expansion overseas.

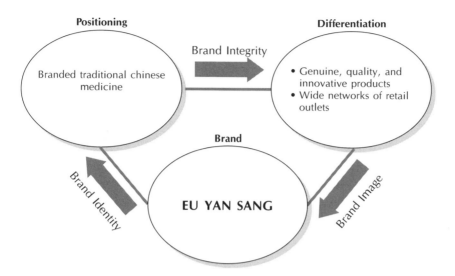

Figure 6.4   Positioning-differentiation-brand triangle of Eu Yan Sang

Black Canyon

During the Asian financial crisis, one company in Thailand went against the tide by expanding its business in places where many people dared not tread at that time. The far-sighted entrepreneurial food chain saw beyond the impermanent economic downturn and took a calculated chance to position its coffee houses in prime locations around the country. Established in 1993, Black Canyon (Thailand) Co. Ltd. is now enjoying the fruits of that gamble. Black Canyon shops can be found in over 100 locations in Bangkok and other cities in Thailand, and is now branching overseas as part of a long-term regionalization expansion plan.

Exposure to successful US fast foods and American-style products encouraged the founders, Dr. Thanong Bidaya and Mr. Pravit Chitnarapong, to create an old West cowboy theme for Black Canyon. Its very first coffee house in Central Plaza Ramindra was opened as an 1800s saloon, complete with a bar, clapboard side, and wall-mounted saddles. Its tagline "Black Canyon Coffee: A drink from paradise ... available on earth" was inspired by French orator Talleyrand's famous words, "The best coffee is as black as the devil, hot as hell, pure as an angel and sweet as love!"

The adventurous and energetic coffee chain with double-digit annual growth adds approximately 12 new shops each year in major shopping centers, nationwide superstores, convention centers, entertainment complexes, hospitals, train stations, and airports. In March 2002, the government-owned SME (small and medium-sized enterprise) Venture Capital Fund acquired a 15% equity stake in the company, providing investment for further expansion internationally. In addition to four outlets in Malaysia, four in Indonesia and one each in Singapore, Cambodia, and Myanmar, Black Canyon has recently entered into the Middle East market with four branches and plans to open more.

Black Canyon operates three types of outlets—full restaurants, mini-restaurants, and kiosks under the Black Canyon X'press name in several stations of Bangkok's commuter train system. Some of the outlets are owned and operated by Black Canyon while others are owned and managed by franchisees. All outlets are similarly decorated to the same high standards and tasteful design variations to suit the specific location. Customer satisfaction and quality service rank as the highest priority and Black Canyon makes all efforts to ensure that customers keep coming back to enjoy their favorite cuppa.

In 2004, Thailand's largest coffee house chain received the Superbrands award for being one of the strongest brands in the country. Black Canyon's excellent reputation is earned by serving coffee of the highest quality, with the best aroma and taste, made from 100% fresh coffee beans from the best plantations in the world. This includes the highest grade of pure Arabica coffee beans grown by hill tribes in northern Thailand under the Royal Patronage of His Majesty the King. A variety of coffee beverages to suit individual tastes can be expected in every outlet—from traditional blacks to iced mocha, from kahlua-flavored Mexican to Black Canyon's signature coffee blended with a ten-year-old secret recipe. Freshness is always guaranteed by master roasters and experienced *baristas* who monitor and control every batch of coffee before sending it out to the retail outlets.

To complement its coffees, dining customers can enjoy cuisines from the best of East and West. Dishes include a spread of traditional Thai and popular international meals so that there is something for everyone. Diners can choose from the wide variety of local fried rice, spicy salads, sandwiches, and grilled steaks, or fusion dishes such as Italian pasta with green curry sauce and Japanese udon noodles in tom-yum soup. Tasty delicious food must also be healthy and nutritious and Black Canyon prepares all its dishes with the finest natural ingredients, herbs, and spices straight from the source without flavor enhancers. Whether one is entertaining business colleagues or having a family meal together, eating at Black Canyon is a totally unique and refreshing experience. The menu is specially designed in a magazine format called *The Magazine Twin Menu.* Customers can find full-colored photographs along with helpful descriptions and interesting facts about the food items. All food and drinks are reasonably priced to suit the local customers in line with the company's value-for-money principle.

New products and seasonal promotions are launched regularly to generate vibrancy and fun. The Coffee Lover Privilege Card entitles card members special discounts on food and beverages at all Black Canyon branches. The "One Dish & One Drink" promotion gives customers a special discount when ordering newly introduced dishes with selected drinks. In months such as February, all coffee houses feature the "Month of Love" promotion and during September's Vegetarian Festival, a special vegetarian menu is available. Brand awareness plays an important part of Black Canyon's marketing program. The company actively partners with leading mobile phone network providers and major banks to cosponsor both private and public events and popular TV shows.

Black Canyon is not afraid to change and explore new ground. It updated its logo from a respectful elderly cowboy to a younger coffee-drinking cowboy wearing a sheriff's star badge to appeal to the younger generation of coffee drinkers and diners. The physical and international expansion of the coffee chain also includes broadening its operation from coffee house and restaurant to bakery. "My Bread" targets the middle-class and young customer segment and was set up after extensive research on the industry.

The resourceful company continues to reinvent itself locally as well as make its mark in overseas markets. The wide choice of Thai dishes on its menu distinguishes Black Canyon from other franchised coffee shops. Its indoor and outdoor outlets in other countries are decorated to the taste of the local patrons in different regions to ensure the best comfort of the customers. The Thai Department of Export Promotion presented Black Canyon with the Thailand Brand credential as a guarantee that their overseas branches serve authentic Thai food. In addition, Black Canyon participated in the government-led Thai restaurant franchise venture to Europe, US, the Middle East, and Asia to promote Thailand as "The World's Kitchen." The fast-growing network in the Middle East is evident of the imminent success in global franchising for Black Canyon.

The positioning of Black Canyon as a food house that unifies West and East is solidly differentiated by its unique combination of extensive Western and Asian food and coffee menu. The Wild West

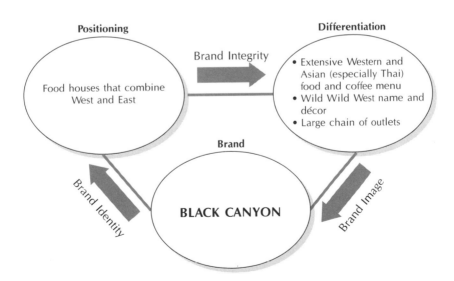

Figure 6.5   Positioning-differentiation-brand triangle of Black Canyon

décor, restaurant name, and cowboy symbol further reflect and apply the Western context to its Asian content. Spurred by its determination to ride into new territories, the iconic Wild West Asian coffee house chain is seen across the region. The success of Black Canyon at home is exported to neighboring countries and markets that share similar Asian tastes and inclination to Wild West flair and fare.

Lessons Learned

The companies discussed in this chapter have similar characteristics that allow them to expand overseas by adopting their respective strategic business triangle models to the new markets.

First, all these companies display strong distribution networks for their products and services, a prerequisite for establishing regional brands. Extra Joss and San Miguel depend on widespread availability of their products as their infrastructure differentiation. Royal Selangor, Eu Yan Sang, and Black Canyon have a significant number of outlets to sustain their brand presence as well as to ensure accessibility and convenience for their customers.

The second characteristic is "transferability." In the previous chapter, the cases show that the export of home brands is, in part, based on transferability of unique product qualities to host markets. In this chapter, the cases demonstrate that regional expansion is executed by transferring the attributes of their strategic business triangle. Rather than counting on niche value propositions which will create barriers for expansion into new markets, these companies sought to leverage on their home superiority and apply the general approaches for expansion.

The third is the importance of brand building. Without first achieving a credible and strong domestic brand, expanding overseas will be an uphill effort with little benefits derived from the regional presence. Therefore brand building and regional expansion must work in tandem, each contributing to and building on the success of the other.

chapter 7

Be Inspired by Multinationals Focusing on ASEAN

Globalization thus reflects a special, and rather unusual, outcome of doing international business, and regional strategies are more relevant than global ones.[1]

Alan Rugman

Not many companies are truly global. Instead, most companies are usually strong only in some regions in the world and thus maintain a regional focus. The regional scale that provides profitable opportunities and regional scope that contains manageable threats make regional markets the best markets to target.

ASEAN countries have been particularly successful in attracting multinationals from Asia to use the region as a springboard into the world, and for multinationals outside Asia to take the region as a gateway to the East. ASEAN was also part of the flying geese formation and the industrialization wave that started in Japan and Korea in the 1970s. To the multinationals focusing here, ASEAN is where they can be successful in implementing their strategic goals of expansion and brand building.

Multinationals coming into ASEAN see it as a cost-effective, resource-rich and politically stable production base, as well as an enormous consumer market. The relationships between the multinationals and ASEAN customers are deeply rooted and have taken time to develop. For a start, many of the brands available today are no strangers to ASEAN

---

[1] Alan M. Rugman and Alain Verbeke, "Regional and Global Strategies of Multinational Enterprises," *Journal of International Business Studies*, Vol. 35, No. 1, 2004.

customers. This is because the companies have been here for years providing jobs and using local products and services for their factories and representative offices. The brand presence has already entered the countries way before the products are sold at stores here.

In this chapter, we look at three very different companies—3M, Kinokuniya Books, and Samsung Electronics. Each case will show the different approaches taken to market their brands to ASEAN customers. Their presence in this region and continued investment in this area reveal the market strength and commitment of ASEAN as a business hub for MNCs all over the world.

The first case shows how one of the world's well-known brands, 3M, builds its strategic business triangle on the foundation of diversity and innovation. The company's product diversity is its principal strength, and innovation through technology is its key enabler.

3M

Everyone in the world is a customer of 3M one way or another. The American corporation originally known as Minnesota Mining and Manufacturing Company (until 2002) produces over 55,000 products, including adhesives, abrasives, laminates, passive fire protection, electronic circuits and displays, and pharmaceuticals. It was incorporated in 1902 by five businessmen who had hoped to build a lucrative materials trading company but almost went bankrupt a few years later from errors in their products and production. The early misadventures inculcated the "never say die" corporate attitude that only ingenuity and perseverance can overcome even potentially ruinous mistakes. From a US$500 laboratory in 1916 to US$1.24 billion on research and development, or 6% of its revenue in 2005,[2] 3M is indeed a true innovation-driven company.

Each year, the company introduces over 500 new products that can be used in almost any aspect of our environment—in our homes, schools, offices, transportation, and hospitals, all with the same intent

---

[2] Michael Arndt, "3M's Seven Pillars of Innovation," *BusinessWeek*, May 10, 2006.

of making our daily lives easier and better. The 3M "ideas factory" holds about 600 patents issued by the US and has R&D centers all over the world. The company's innovation culture dutifully handed down from the founding leaders to the newest employee today is based on the "The Seven Habits of Highly Innovative Corporations" as listed below:

1. From the chief executive on down, the company must be committed to innovation.
2. The corporate culture must be actively maintained.
3. Innovation is impossible without a broad base of technology.
4. Talk, talk, talk.
5. Set individual expectations and reward employees for outstanding work.
6. Quantify efforts.
7. Research must be tied to the customer.

The company has more than 35 business units, organized into six major sectors—consumer and office; display and graphics; electronics and communications; healthcare; industrial and transportation; and safety, security, and protection services. This allows the company to provide an extensive range of solutions for automotive, communication arts, construction and maintenance, consumer, electronics/electrical, healthcare, industrial, office, pharmaceutical, telecommunications, transportation, safety and security markets, and space exploration. In 2005, 3M's worldwide sales in more than 200 countries exceeded US$21 billion with international sales accounting for 61% of that total. The number of employees has grown proportionately to 69,000 of which 36,000 work in branches outside the US and serve the local markets directly.

3M's overseas expansion began in 1929 to Europe and in Asia, as early as 1951 to Australia. In 1966, 3M started in a small rented office in Singapore with eight employees. The following year, the company established its Malaysian branch with nine employees sharing a 1,500 sq ft room and all its inventories. In the same year, 3M Thailand opened in a similar unassuming manner in its main city Bangkok. In 1973, 3M set up a factory in the Philippines to manufacture masking, cellophane, transparent, and packaging tapes as the initial products. 3M Indonesia started in 1975 to bring the wide range of products and services to the local marketplace. 3M Vietnam, established in 1994 in Ho Chi Minh City, became the 61st international 3M subsidiary.

As 3M experienced steady growth worldwide, the ASEAN branches began to expand from their nondescript offices to bigger premises to acquired buildings, large manufacturing plants, and state-of-the-art research centers. The company's investments into the region increased with the emerging markets in the Asia Pacific and the excellent cost-effective production bases in the developing countries. ASEAN management and employees adopt the same innovative and customer-oriented corporate culture that is characteristic of 3M. Over the years, they have succeeded in producing, promoting, and distributing quality products as well as the outstanding brand in this part of the world.

The Singapore subsidiary is also the Asia-Pacific headquarters employing over 700 people responsible for 15 countries in the region such as Bangladesh, Brunei, Nepal, and the Maldives. In 1994 3M invested S$11 million to build the Innovation Center which houses 15 applications laboratories today, with over 70 engineers and scientists working on the latest innovations and high value-added research and design activities. Residing in the northern part of Singapore in Woodlands industrial estate is one of 3M's largest factories outside the US and one of three in the world. The S$400 million 550,000 sq ft advanced manufacturing facility produces Microflex Circuits for inkjet cartridges and hard disk drives.

Across the Causeway in nearby Malaysia, 3M was expanding so rapidly that it had to be relocated to bigger premises with proper warehousing facilities in Ampang, Kuala Lumpur in just over three months after its establishment. By 1971, extensive renovations were carried out to accommodate rapid growth and the subsequent increase in employees. Eventually, the entire warehousing and distribution were consolidated into a huge complex near the country's international airport in the Subang Jaya area. From the main office in Petaling Jaya, 3M Malaysia oversees the extension operations in the country including its main manufacturing facility located at an industrial park in Seremban, a southwestern town which produces a host of products for the local market and international exports.

3M's model in Thailand is similar to Malaysia's. Its Bangkok office manages the sales and marketing functions in the country, as well as the warehousing operations and manufacturing of various tapes, adhesives, abrasives, and decorative graphic film for automotives such as decals, tags, labels, fleet graphics, nameplates, and graphic overlays.

In the Philippines, the company sells about 10,000 products, most of which are being manufactured or converted locally such as printed box sealing tapes, flexible adhesives, contact cements (ceramics and vinyl adhesives), floor finish chemicals, rubbing compounds, rubberized automotive under-seal coating, and traffic control materials. With a staff strength of about 200, the central Makati City office manages all plant facilities, distribution networks, and sub-branches in Cebu, Bacolod, and Davao.

Besides manufacturing and distributing the main consumer products, 3M Indonesia is particularly active in coming up with innovative product applications for car makers based in Indonesia such as Toyota Kijang and Isuzu. In 1997, the Automotive Design Systems Division produced a new body side molding for car interiors using Vitrotrim™ and Acrylic Foam Tape 4229. From 1998, all operations were consolidated in the Tambun Bekasi factory while sales and marketing offices remain in the three major cities of Jakarta, Bandung, and Surabaya.

As Vietnam investment laws require licenses for manufacturing, processing, and assembly processes based in the country, 3M Vietnam is permitted to conduct business for certain products in the electrical distribution, telecommunications, medical, dental, graphics, automotive care/finishing, and traffic control materials. All other 3M products are serviced from its representative office with support from the Singapore regional headquarters. With the growing Vietnamese economy, 3M built a factory in Cat Lai Industrial Zone and is present in the two major cities, Ho Chi Minh City and Hanoi.

The company's success in ASEAN from the early industrialization era in Asia gave it a strong foundation for expansion into the rest of

Asia to Korea, China, and India. The online game "3M Everywhere" has a deeper connotation than just to promote brand awareness beyond the popular Scotch® and Post-it® products. It reinforces the company's seven pillars of innovation that one does not need a specific time and place to innovate. Rather, innovation should happen all the time by anyone everywhere whenever there is an opportunity to make things work better, solve problems, and improve the lives and safety of fellow human beings.

When the company celebrated a Century of Innovation, it celebrated the generations of imaginative, industrious, and talented 3M employees in all parts of the organization all around the world.

3M's positioning of diverse innovation is a unique one as it encompasses a wide spectrum of products and technologies that are linked together with a simple philosophy of making lives better. Innovation leads to progress and ASEAN customers are eager to be involved with innovation and progress. Companies such as 3M that endorse innovation in its strategic business triangle are readily accepted. The key lesson is not to relate your strategic business triangle to innovation alone but to any issue that connects with the customers

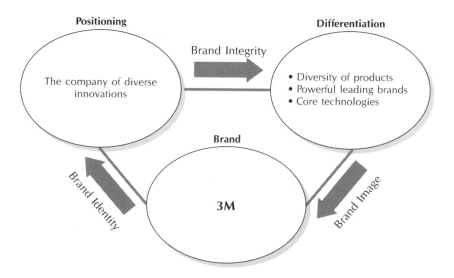

Figure 7.1   Positioning-differentiation-brand triangle of 3M

in the region. Although 3M is a global company, the level of acceptance in a particular region will still depend on how it is able to connect to its regional customers.

The next case, Kinokuniya, gives a different inspiration in its positioning-differentiation-brand triangle where the largest Japanese bookstore chain shows its sensitivity to cultural issues in its content and context differentiation.

Kinokuniya

To a book lover, Kinokuniya is like a giant candy store to a child. The only difference is that one gets to taste the enticing contents on the shelves without purchasing them first. The grand dame of contemporary book stores has never failed to impress and delight everyone who has stepped inside its enormous shops filled with all kinds of books, some of which are exhibited like curious works of art. Founded in 1927, Kinokuniya is the leading bookstore chain in Japan with 58 domestic and 22 overseas stores. To attain a high level of customer satisfaction, the company has been opening large-scale bookstores, selling publications over the Internet, and building up a peerless network of sales offices serving educational and research institutions all over the world.

In true Japanese custom, Kinokuniya takes great pride and effort to ensure that all their customers get what they want, literally. The massive selection of magazines, journals, books, comics, and specialized professional publications can be found in English, Japanese, and other native languages such as Malay, Bahasa Indonesia, Thai, French, and German. From its first store in the Shinjuku district of Tokyo, a thriving shopping area that surrounds a major train station, Kinokuniya stores around the world are always located in prime, easily accessible shopping malls.

Following the completion of its headquarters building in 1964, Kinokuniya expanded to all major Japanese cities and opened its first overseas bookstore in San Francisco in 1969. The move overseas was meant to serve the twin goals of providing Japanese living abroad with information from home as quickly as possible and introducing Japanese tradition and culture to the local community. Since then,

Kinokuniya has opened several other bookstores in the US, including major stores in Los Angeles and New York. The first store in Asia was at Liang Court shopping center in Singapore where it introduced a whole new book shopping experience in 1983. The success of the Singapore store led to the opening of more Asian outlets in Taiwan, Indonesia, Malaysia, Thailand, and Australia.

With customer service close to heart, Kinokuniya views itself as a service provider of knowledge and the joy of discovery. The company is like a stage, books and information products are like actors and actresses, store personnel are like producers and directors, and customers are like the audience. Once the customers come into contact with Kinokuniya, their theatrical experience begins. To receive a standing ovation from the customers, the book store must provide a well-designed stage. The staff must provide clear directions to the actors and actresses and they must ensure all props are in place. Actors and actresses are well cared for so that they can perform their very best before the audience. This corporate philosophy keeps the shopping experience alive and inter-active. No longer are books silent aloof sentinels in cold quiet places. At Kinokuniya, the children's books area is as exciting as a toy store; the magazines corner is like an adult playground as enthusiasts indulge in their own secret passions; and the business section is like a virtual convention where world-class gurus talk directly to keen apprentices.

One of the most frequented parts of the store is the information counter where well-trained and polite staff proficiently answers enquiries, takes reservations, and guides the shopper to the exact shelf which holds the requested book. Behind the prompt and excellent service is Kinokuniya's massive database and real-time inventory management system. This is connected to its point-of-sale terminals where sales data is captured immediately for automated ordering and restocking. Linked to this is the online book-ordering service, BookWeb, which combines the convenience of online shopping with familiarity of the local stores. With immediate Internet access to real stock, BookWeb aims to differentiate itself from other online book web sites.

Kinokuniya encourages its stores in different countries to use creative local marketing to promote to different market segments.

For example, Singapore's flagship store in Ngee Ann City organizes frequent multicultural activities such as *ikebana* demonstrations, comic art illustrations, language workshops, Japanese tea appreciation, and book launches to cater to both local and international shoppers along Orchard Road in its massive 43,000 sq ft location. The revamped 14,000 sq ft Liang Court store boasts a Chinese book section and Japanese stationery and bargain section, in addition to the wide range of English and Japanese books. Its Bugis Junction store is filled with comics and travel, language, new age, and leisure books targeted at the younger crowd, mostly young executives and students in the popular entertainment and shopping complex. To date Kinokuniya has three stores in Thailand, the newest one in the upmarket mega mall called Siam Paragon; one in Malaysia's premier shopping center at Suria Kuala Lumpur Convention Center next to the famous Petronas twin towers; and two in Jakarta, Indonesia.

Along with its retail business, Kinokuniya provides a comprehensive information service to libraries, academic institutions, and research organizations through its next-generation library support system. This system supports a professional version of BookWeb called BookWeb Pro, a centralized acquisition and management system known as New Platon, an operations support outsourcing system, an online computer library center, an online database, and a journal access service. Professional bodies are finding this service incredibly useful as they are able to streamline their operations and maintain efficient library systems. The relationship between the bookstore and its corporate consumers is intimately linked as both share the same requirements in managing large collections of publications. Because of this, Kinokuniya is well positioned to address the needs of its customers and is able to differentiate itself from other book suppliers.

Whether one is shopping for books in Plaza Senayan in Jakarta or in the Tokyo Metropolitan area, Kinokuniya will offer the same buying pleasure and excellent service that make customers return to the store over and over again to be entertained and enlightened by knowledge. Through years of research and dedicated sourcing of in-demand publications, Kinokuniya has successfully remained competitive and progressive in offering customers the best in book experience.

The positioning of Kinokuniya is different from other bookstores in the world. ASEAN customers perceive Kinokuniya as the leading provider of both information and cultural publications with its large categories of books and other types of reading materials. The book-buying experience and large network of bookshops serve as its context differentiation.

As a region where culture is important, ASEAN is an ideal target market for Kinokuniya. The style of presenting books in an experiential way suits the growing sophistication of the new-age readers in the region. Kinokuniya has clearly understood the regional socio-cultural trends and succeeded in applying its strategic business triangle to this region.

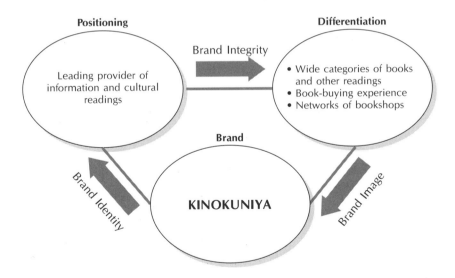

Figure 7.2 Positioning-differentiation-brand triangle of Kinokuniya

Similarly, Samsung presents another lesson in formulating the right strategic business triangle overseas. The company is not afraid to challenge and beat its rivals as the market leader of consumer electronics. Here's how Samsung made its mark in the region and in the world.

Samsung

"With the start of the second millennium, Samsung begins its second century." That was the unpretentious, realistic pitch at the future by the Korean giant that had just undergone a major restructuring with massive reductions in affiliated companies and employees, and sold ten business units to overseas companies in late 1999 in order to stay afloat. True to its tenacious spirit to turn the company around, Samsung focused on building a more upscale image through better quality, design, and innovation of what it does best—digital technology.

At the crossroads to becoming a world leader or a major failure six years ago, Samsung had a once-in-a-lifetime shot when it went the digital route. In 2001 the newly defined Samsung came out with rapid launches of new lines of top-notch mobile phones that created a frenzy of brand bonding first in its home country and soon with the rest of the world. Though the flashy gadgets were instrumental in branding Samsung worldwide, they were actually loss leaders. The bulk of Samsung's profits came from churning out some of the world's most advanced digital components, from flash memory chips to LCD screens. Currently, Samsung's products that have dominated the world's market share include dynamic random access memory (DRAM), color cathode-ray tube TVs, TFT-LCD glass substrates, CDMA handsets, flash memory, LCD Driver IC (LDI), plasma display panel (PDP) modules, PCB for handhelds (mobile phone plates), flame retardant ABS, and dimethyl formamide (DMF).

In 2005 Samsung was named one of the fastest-growing brands by Interbrand in the Global 100 ranking of brand valuation. Korea's most famous company achieved the biggest gain in value with a 186% surge in the recent five years, beating its biggest and most established competitor, Sony. Samsung's ascent to the league of top global companies is evident by the fact that its brand value has grown in the past five years—43rd (US$5.2 billion) in 2000, 42nd (US$6.4 billion) in 2001, 34th (US$8.3 billion) in 2002, 25th (US$10.8 billion) in 2003, 21st (US$12.5 billion) in 2004, and 20th (US$14.9 billion) in 2005.

The former "back of the store" brand of bulky TVs and boom boxes has come a long way. Founded in 1938 by former chairman

Byung-Chull Lee with only 30,000 won or US$32, Lee's little business of selling dried Korean fish, vegetables, and fruits to Manchuria and Beijing grew into one of the world's largest consumer electronics and diversified groups. Samsung, which means "three stars" in Korean, is a far-reaching enterprise which had its sights on the global market early. From the 1970s, the company positioned itself in the promising home electronics business in both domestic and export markets. In 1974, it entered into the budding semiconductor industry by acquiring a 50% stake in an existing Korean semiconductor manufacturer. Subsequently, it developed the successful 64K DRAM very large-scale integration (VLSI) chip which paved the way forward for Samsung to become a world leader in semiconductor products.

On the 50th anniversary of Samsung's founding in 1988, the founder's son and present chairman, Kun-Hee Lee, announced the "Second Foundation" and directed the company to be a world-class 21st century corporation. The visionary leader consolidated the electronics, semiconductor, and telecommunications business in order to maximize its technological resources and develop value-added products for the world. At a time when digital convergence and infocomm technologies (ICT) were unheard of, Lee's pioneering force and clarity in strategic management steered Samsung way ahead of its present and future competitors into what we now know as an infinite global digital market.

In the 1970s and 80s Japanese firms such as Toshiba, Sony, and Sanyo ruled the consumer electronics industries with Korean companies basically adopting a "follow the leader" strategy. When Goldstar, another Korean electronics company moved into Thailand, Samsung followed right behind in 1987. Samsung's first TV assembly plant in Thailand spurred its rapid overseas expansion to other parts of Asia. In 1991 Samsung started a purchasing office in Singapore to speed up the internationalization of production and to coordinate supplies of low-cost parts for its Korean-based production sites.

By 1995, Samsung ASEAN subsidiaries in Thailand, Indonesia, Malaysia, and Vietnam were producing color TVs, refrigerators, washing machines, microwave ovens, and electronic parts such as transformers and deflection yokes. Within ten years, production expanded from making household appliances to office electronics, memory chips, mobile phones, IT products, and LCD panels. The introduction of the mobile handset business in 1999 launched Samsung into the highly dynamic telecommunications industry to become the second largest mobile phone company in the Asia Pacific. Its international procurement remains in Singapore which is also its regional headquarters employing a total of 6,400 people in seven countries and 11 entities in ASEAN and Australia.

At the turn of the 21st century globalization and digitization brought about revolutionary opportunities and changes to the world of business. In the digital era, creativity and speed have become the most important factors. With shorter product lifecycles due to faster technology advancements, product development and the supply chain have to be faster in order to respond efficiently in the global markets. Samsung's outstanding performance lies in its ability to move swiftly and coherently in three key areas—R&D, organization, and production, emerging as one of the world's top ten companies in US patents with 13,000 researchers representing a US$1.7 billion investment in R&D of leading-edge and embryonic technologies.

The challenge in responding to rapid technological changes is being faced by all companies, including Samsung's competitors. Instead of fighting head on, the Korean giant supplies memory chips to Apple for the new iPod Nano, even though it sells its own MP3 players. Similarly, Samsung supplies most of the flash memory used at Nokia, components that go into the Sony PlayStation and LCDs for Sony's TVs. Samsung's view is that this type of competitor-supplier arrangement is inevitable in the digital era because no one can cope with the changes alone. The multifaceted relationship allows Samsung to excel in technological competence while riding on its competitor's brand equity.

Samsung's goal is to be ranked among the world's top three digital technology companies by the year 2010. It is already one of the largest corporations in Korea. In terms of export, Samsung took up 18.1% of the national export amount with US$31.2 billion in 2000 and 20.7% with US$52.7 billion in 2004. The enterprising Korean corporation is the only company that integrates the core competencies of digital technology—LCD panels, memory (DRAM, Flash, etc.), digital media (A/V and IT), digital appliances, and telecommunications—into a single business operation for the home and office and mobile environments.

With over a decade's experience in ICT, Samsung is definitely leading in its dominance in the digital world by being able to position itself inside and outside consumer products. The convoluted partnerships with its ostensible competitors may seem radical today, but so was its decision to converge its electronics, semiconductor, and telecommunications business in the 1980s. That is what makes a true leader—one that can see beyond the present, visualize the future, and be committed in the quest to succeed in realizing the vision.

Samsung's foremost positioning promotes the company as a formidable player in a world that is moving toward digital convergence. Its content and context differentiation comes in the form of its wide range of trendy products equipped with astonishing features and functionalities. Many ASEAN countries are early adopters of consumer electronic technologies. The ability of Samsung to drive the market toward digital convergence makes it extremely successful in the region.

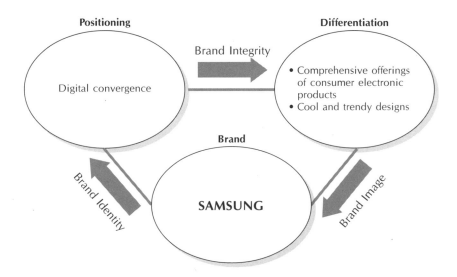

Figure 7.3   Positioning-differentiation-brand triangle of Samsung

Lessons Learned

From the three cases, we learn the different approaches that companies can take in building their positioning-differentiation-brand strategies. Each strategy is unique. So what are the reasons for their successes in ASEAN?

First, a brand must be linked to a real and topical issue in the region. 3M connects with ASEAN with its innovation, Kinokuniya with its experiential shopping, and Samsung with its digital convergence. Second, multinational companies must understand the socio-cultural behavior of their foreign customers. Customers in any particular region possess a similar set of values and behavior. You can relate to your positioning-differentiation-brand model and match these for maximum acceptance in regional markets. Third, multinational giants focusing on particular regions must be positioned to drive the market. Being a developing market, ASEAN is more ready and willing to accept new things. That is why new and novel products and services are always welcomed in these vibrant markets.

Part **III**

ASEAN Marketing in Practice

Marketing in general is about identifying markets and providing the most appropriate methods to optimize from these markets. Marketing in abstract is about creating, promoting, and preserving a company's most important value—its brand.

Together with people, processes, and inventions, a company's brand is part of its intangible assets. Physical infrastructures are easily rebuilt if destroyed but intangible assets are the "software" of the company, and the brand is its currency. A company's performance is therefore tied very closely to its brand. According to Interbrand, an international branding consultant, "brand value" is calculated as the net present value of a company's earnings that the brand is expected to generate and secure in the future for a specific time frame.

In Part II, we have demonstrated the significance of the positioning-differentiation-brand triangle to an organization's strategy, tactic, and overall value. This triangle, also referred to as strategy-tactic-value triangle (STV) can be further expanded to explain how the three interrelated self-reinforcing components actually form the basis of the strategic business triangle. In the book *Rethinking Marketing*, we defined the nine core elements of the triangle as segmentation, targeting, positioning, differentiation, marketing mix, selling, brand, service, and process.

Segmentation, targeting, and positioning form the marketing strategy to win the customers' mind share. Differentiation, marketing mix, and selling form the marketing tactic to capture market share. Tactics are normally localized to achieve greater effectiveness while strategies are implemented as guiding rules to win business. Brand, service, and process are the values of the company. This is what the company gives to its customers, and what the customers perceive they are receiving from the products and services.

The nine core elements hold the company together and none of these should ever break down or be displaced. Any failure or degradation of any of these elements will create adverse results in the company's performance. For example, if the service quality falls, it will affect the brand which makes it difficult for salespeople to sell no matter how much the company spends on advertisements or how accurate the target market has been defined. Companies serious about doing well must take the STV model seriously.

In the following chapters, you will read about successful companies which have implemented STV effectively and have made remarkable gains from these approaches. All five cases featured have completely different products and services addressing different markets and they come from totally different backgrounds. Of the five, three are mature established brands—Toyota Kijang, Hewlett-Packard, and Yamaha—while two, AirAsia and BreakTalk, are relatively young ASEAN companies with crystal clear visions of making home their first regional market.

chapter **8**

ASEAN Vision, Local Action

One size doesn't fit all.

Anonymous

It is commonly said that charity begins at home. This is the same with business. Local success will always pave the way to regional and international achievements. The home country makes the best testing ground and most dependable showcase for any company with a vision to expand to new foreign markets. Once a company has established its brand, market positioning, and product differentiation in its own domestic market, the same model can be emulated overseas by adapting and localizing the variables within the strategic business triangle.

To win in the ASEAN market, companies must make extra effort to understand the similarities and differences in the neighboring countries, independently as well as an integrated whole. Balancing standardization and localization is the key to successful regionalization strategies. This involves the close examination and implementation of the strategies to win mind share, local tactics to win market share, and branding value to win heart share. All core elements of the strategy-tactic-value (STV) triangle comes into play in realizing an ASEAN vision and local action.

At the end of the day, customers must feel that the products and services they are buying are of value to them, that the companies owning the brands have created something different and special to meet their needs, and that they can always rely on going back for more. That is brand value.

In this chapter, we will share with you three companies that are successful in their home countries and are equally successful in foreign lands. They have succeeded by paying great attention to what the locals want, and by creating for themselves high brand values.

AirAsia
"Now Everyone Can Fly."

Tony Fernandes, the Chief Executive Officer of AirAsia, is the undeniable personality and icon for low-cost carriers (LCCs) in Asia. After graduating from the London School of Economics in 1987, the 23-year-old Malaysian worked as an accountant for Richard Branson's Virgin Records and went on to become Vice-President for Warner Music Group Southeast Asia until 2001 before realizing his childhood dream of running an airline. Without any prior involvement with airlines whatsoever, the charismatic entrepreneur had only two qualifications—knowing what budget air travelers want and knowing exactly what makes a business profitable.

In October 2001, Fernandes successfully convinced then Prime Minister Mahathir Mohamad to start Malaysia's first discount airline that could revolutionize Southeast Asian air travel and boost tourism at a time when the travel industry was struggling from the impact of the September 11 terrorist attacks. Through his newly incorporated company, Tune Air Sdn. Bhd., Fernandes paid a token US 27 cents (one Malaysian ringgit) for bankrupt government-owned AirAsia with two aging Boeing jets and US$11 million in debt.

AirAsia's re-entry into the market was a real test of guts when established airlines were retrenching staff and reducing routes due to spiraling operations costs and a drop in the number of air travelers. Fernandes, however, saw this as perfect timing—aircraft leasing costs were down 40%; airline layoffs meant experienced staff was readily available; and travelers would embrace a cut-rate air service that will save time and money in a tight economy. The budget airline's mission was to make flying affordable for everyone, something unheard of in the region. At that time, the aviation industry was dominated by traditional full-cost carriers (FCCs) which competed on bigger seats, wider leg room, exotic cuisines, and state-of-the-art in-flight entertainment. But the unimaginable happened—within two years of operation, AirAsia showed profits for the first time and proved that a no-frills airline model actually works.

With the changing demands of consumers, AirAsia has skillfully created new untapped markets of travelers who could not afford to fly before. Due to rising living standards and household incomes, the presence of LCCs makes air travel accessible to the wider public. Being the first to introduce low fares, AirAsia generates widespread goodwill as a bearer of good news to many travelers. To date the AirAsia group has carried over 10 million passengers and is expected to carry eight million passengers in 2006 alone. With one-way fares as low as US$2.50, thousands of Asians who in the past would have taken a bus, train, or boat, are now persuaded to fly.

Fernandes' biggest achievement has been to turn AirAsia into a regional low-cost carrier. Before he arrived on the scene, countries in the region never had any kind of open-skies agreement. In mid-2003, Fernandes' lobbying pushed Mahathir to raise the idea with the leaders of neighboring Thailand and Indonesia. As a result, these countries have granted landing rights to AirAsia and other discount carriers. AirAsia has effectively changed the airline industry in the Asia Pacific. It now operates more than 100 domestic and international flights daily to 52 areas in Malaysia and eight other Asian countries—Thailand, Indonesia, the Philippines, Singapore, Brunei, Cambodia, Macau, and China. The fleet of aircraft has expanded from the original two to 41.

To raise funds for future expansion, the energetic airline successfully raised RM717.4 million (US$197 million) in a public listing on the Malaysia Stock Exchange (Bursa Malaysia) in 2004. In line with its growth plans, AirAsia secured a 100-aircraft commitment from Airbus for its A320s (60 firm orders, 40 options), which will place the budget carrier as the single largest customer for the aircraft in the Asia Pacific, and potentially one of the largest airline fleets in the region. The new aircraft would gradually replace AirAsia's existing Boeing 737-300s.

In 2004, AirAsia formed a partnership with one of Thailand's largest conglomerates, Shin Corporation, to develop a low-fare carrier, Thai AirAsia based in Bangkok. Besides serving the domestic routes, the Thai operations introduced a flight from Bangkok to the Special Administrative Region (SAR) of Macau. Subsequently AirAsia launched its maiden service to Macau from its hub in Kuala Lumpur, the first low-fare airline to do so. In the same year, it bought a stake in an Indonesian private airline, PT AWAIR, and launched Indonesian AirAsia for domestic routes to Bali, Medan, and Padang from the Soekarno-Hatta International Airport in Jakarta.

AirAsia kept its costs low with short-haul flights, a high rate of aircraft utilization, and a fast turnaround rate. Income is derived from the sales of tickets and food and drinks on board, a lucrative cargo service, and marketing tie-ups with other companies. The low-fare no-frills airline recorded profits of US$5.2 million within 20 months of operation, US$13.5 million in 2004, and US$30.6 million in 2005.

A new budget terminal, the first of its kind in Southeast Asia, opened in Sepang near Kuala Lumpur on March 23, 2006. Built at a cost of RM108 million (US$29.2 million) and spanning 35,000 sq m, it has the capacity to handle 30,000 passengers daily and is the new home for AirAsia.

The phenomenal growth of AirAsia reflects its vision to become an ASEAN brand by being the epitome of ASEAN with its rich cultures and wealth of resources. In AirAsia, branding starts internally with the staff. The company feels that without the staff understanding the branding of a company, it is unlikely that externally focused branding exercises would work. All AirAsia staff must first know the company's direction and have the "will to win" attitude before any effort is made to convince others.

A motivated and empowered workforce will serve the customers better and engage in various ways to improve the company's efficiency and profitability. AirAsia's fun, exciting, and innovative corporate culture is one that resonates from the CEO to flight engineers to the passengers. Being in a borderless world means an open office concept for AirAsia. The "smallest airline office in the world" has no compartmentalization so everyone knows exactly what is going on and can give and receive help whenever required. All staff in the office uses the same entrance and exit to promote a group identity and casual dressing is encouraged to reduce the "power distance" between ranks. In order not to lose sight of the business, the AirAsia office is located at the airport where employees can have hands-on experience such as bag handling and ticketing so that they understand the various aspects of the business and can handle complaints and feedback competently.

Being a low-cost carrier, the cost structure is of utmost importance but this must not come at the expense of customer safety and service. AirAsia controls its costs mainly in fuel consumption, aircraft usage, and in areas where costs do not add value. For example, it understands that the fuel consumption of a plane waiting for take-off will be considerably high at big busy airports where queues are frequent. In most international airports catering to large aircraft, the runways are usually very long which means more fuel will be used for taxiing and taking off. In addition, this adds to the wear and tear of the aircraft and increases maintenance and replacement costs.

AirAsia's preference to operate from secondary and smaller airports also means that they enjoy lower landing and parking fees compared to larger international airports. While other airlines spend money training staff in maintaining many types of aircraft and stocking a large inventory of spare parts, AirAsia concentrates on just two types of plane, the Boeing 737-300 and Airbus 320. This means the technical team can stay focused and become experts in the operations and maintenance of the fleet.

When AirAsia could not sell their tickets through travel agencies (due to the latter's agreements with other national carriers), it used an alternative marketing channel via the Internet. With over three million hits a month, the online www.airasia.com web site is one of the most widely accessed travel sites. Online ticket booking leads to ticketless travel where a customer simply presents his or her identity card or passport for checking in to board flights. This makes traveling much more convenient, helps to keep costs low, and in turn enables AirAsia to keep its airfares low. In August 2003, AirAsia became the first airline in the world to introduce SMS booking. With this service, passengers can book their seats, check flight schedules, and obtain latest updates on AirAsia promotions from the convenience of their mobile phones.

Deviating from the traditional ways of operating an airline helps AirAsia to keep the cost per available seat mile as low as 4 to 5 US cents compared to a full-service airline's cost of 12 to 15 US cents.[1] Although AirAsia had the first mover advantage and has proven the success of the no-frills budget airline model, other low-cost carriers such as Tiger Airways, Valueair, and JetStar appeared quickly to compete for the new pie in the sky. This led to cut-throat price wars and eventually a merger between Valueair and JetStar. Except for AirAsia, all the other low-cost carriers in Asia are still not yet profitable. AirAsia is the leading low-cost carrier simply because of its low-cost structure and stringent cost management. The airline makes no qualms about not offering any in-flight service or allowing for seat reservations but makes up for these by charging low fares and offering friendly air travel experiences to its customers.

The entire vibrant image of the airline is enough to make its low-fare passengers feel welcome and honored every time they walk down the red carpet to their plush leather seats. The attractive and well-trained female crew members in chili-red suits and smart male attendants are genuinely interested in making their guests enjoy the flight with a variety of onboard games and lively conversations. The atmosphere is informal, relaxed, and warm, like being in a familiar place surrounded by friends and people who care. Travelers are seduced by the simple honest charm of AirAsia and are induced by its value offering of safe and comfortable flights.

At the heart of its customer quality service are the six core principles—safety, care, fun, passion, integrity, and the AirAsia experience. The AirAsia experience is a unique blend of professionalism and sincerity of the crew members and the brand that supports the airline. Customers' expectations are properly managed and all staff are kept motivated to do their best for their airline. Good customer relationships are important to forge loyalty where word-of-mouth recommendations are more powerful for the budget airline than incessant costly advertisements.

---

[1] Kapil Kaul, "Less Is More," *FE Business Traveller*, September 2004.

AirAsia's customer relationships do not end just after they complete their journeys. The innovative airline has introduced GO Holiday, an online program that enables guests to book holiday packages, hotel rooms, car rental, and even medical appointments. For a fee, corporations can charter a flight under its special corporate service. The airline's partnership with MasterCard enables AirAsia MasterCard members to enjoy mileage privileges and free flight rewards. The strategy to sponsor the English Premier League Manchester United is to appeal to a different market of tourists to use AirAsia for traveling within Asia. All services, promotional information, and updates can be accessed round the clock from its multilanguage web site in seven languages—English, Mandarin, Malay, Bahasa Indonesia, Tamil, Thai, and Filipino.

CEO Fernandes' vision is to make AirAsia a truly ASEAN brand and the *de facto* low-cost carrier in Asia. The evangelistic Malaysian entrepreneur who professes that low cost is his company's religion has only one simple concept—everyone should be able to fly. Everything AirAsia does, from securing the lowest landing fees to hedging against fluctuating fuel prices, is to make this concept possible by offering the lowest fares to its customers. That is the philosophy of the company and the integrity behind AirAsia's brand name.

With its spot-on positioning as ASEAN's no-frills and fun low-cost carrier, AirAsia has skillfully targeted the low-budget travelers in the travel segment. This is easily applied at home as well as the neighboring countries where the customer needs and traveling profiles are similar. To differentiate from the more sober full-cost carriers, AirAsia presents a fun image from a cheerful aircraft interior to an informal, friendly service for all travelers. Its paperless purchasing system offers hassle-free booking which benefits the airline and its customers by reducing administration and communications costs which in turn results in competitive low-cost pricing. The online system also allows yield management of seat and flight availability as the demand can be monitored in real time and the most competitive pricing can be computed.

To win the hearts of customers outside Malaysia, AirAsia makes every effort to brand itself as a localized airline with Thai AirAsia in

Thailand and Indonesian AirAsia in Indonesia. Its web site "speaks" the native language of the country it operates in, which boasts of being the first in Asia to offer multi-ASEAN language service, besides English and Chinese.

For a young carrier with an ambitious ASEAN vision, AirAsia has strived to prove itself as the airline with an ASEAN Vision and local action.

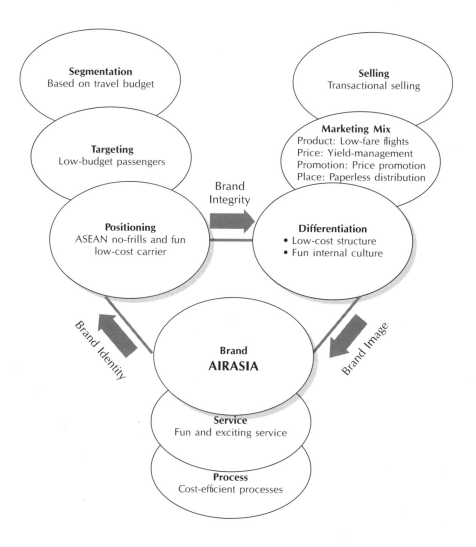

Figure 8.1   Nine core elements of marketing of AirAsia

BreadTalk
Experiential Bakery Boutique

When BreadTalk opened its first retail outlet at Parco Bugis Junction, Singapore in July 2000, long queues formed outside the store, reminiscent of the McDonald's Hello Kitty crowd just a few months into the turn of the millennium. Unlike the "Kitty" craze, BreadTalk fans did not go away. The phenomenal success and growing demand prompted the company to open two more retail stores within five months and another five the following year.

Trailblazer George Quek first conceptualized BreadTalk in April 2000 when he saw an opportunity for starting a bakery selling freshly baked breads and buns which are visually creative and attractive. When one looks at the 200 varieties of breads, buns, pastries, and cakes, each one specially named, it is easy to feel the passion and thoughtfulness that go into all the freshly baked creations. Its continuous development of products to reflect contemporary lifestyles and current events distinguishes BreadTalk from traditional bakeries in the market.

BreadTalk outlets are pretty hard to miss with their urban design and architecture, clear-glass panels, steel and chrome counters, brightly-lit interiors, and neat display shelves filled with "artisanal" breads, cakes, pastries, and buns. In addition, the unique layout of its retail outlets is designed such that customers have a clear view of the bakery items on display and its see-through kitchens allow customers and shoppers to view the staff at work. Store assistants in smart-looking uniforms serve and attend to customers with airline-style promptness and courtesy while bakers dressed like five-star hotel chefs busily turn dough into tasty treats.

Before BreadTalk, no one had ever talked extensively about a bread shopping experience. Buying bread was just a trip to the corner shop—pick one of the usual varieties and head back home. Breads were also not considered as gifts in Asia until BreadTalk revolutionized the culture of bread consumption and introduced a fresh bread appeal. Believe it or not, the award-winning Singaporean bakery boutique wants its breads to "talk" to customers. It is a novel proposal with a deliciously private invitation to everyone who steps into the designer bread shop.

With names like Flosss, Hot Chick, Mt. Fuji Swirl, Sunflower, Moshi Mushroom, and Naan, customers are treated to a totally new multisensory experience in shopping. Signature bread items come in interesting designs, unusual flavors, bizarre shapes, and imaginative names complete with the wonderful aroma of freshly baked breads from the in-house ovens. The real thrill for customers is waiting for their favorite items to come out of the kitchen piping hot and be the first to handpick the freshest breads before they are even displayed on the shelves.

Despite its short track record, BreadTalk has successfully established its brand as the leader in creative bread design and experiential retail shopping. Less than two years from its first launch, the fancy bread creator was presented with the Singapore Promising Brand Award 2002. In the same year, the company clinched Superbrand Status, Singapore Award 2002 and Number 1 of Enterprise 50 Start-up Award 2002. At the Business Design Week 2004: Lifestyle Asia organized by the Hong Kong Design Center, BreadTalk was the only Singapore company to win a Design for Asia Award which recognizes the most commercially effective designs in Asia. In 2005, BreadTalk was voted Singapore's Most Popular Brand in a poll organized jointly by the Association of Small and Medium Enterprises and Singapore Press Holdings.

Lauded as Singapore's favorite son, BreadTalk started to plan for overseas expansion in 2002 using a mixed approach of franchising and wholly owned outlets. Today, it has 24 wholly owned outlets in Singapore and 18 in China, and 27 franchised outlets in Indonesia, Malaysia, Philippines, Hong Kong, Taiwan, Kuwait, and India. BreadTalk provides the brand development while the local partners focus on the network and operations.

For all its overseas outlets, BreadTalk maintains 80% of its product range and adapts 20% to the local palate. For example, a special sweet bread variety called Double Trouble which is puff pastry éclair with custard filling dipped at both ends in rich irresistible chocolate is specially catered to the sweet-loving Filipino market. BreadTalk takes localization seriously by respecting the different local customs, cultures, and dietary requirements. There are vegetarian creations for the health-conscious and the Indian market, breads with *halal* ingredients for the Muslim countries, and savory varieties for the Chinese populated markets.

"Innovation is the bread and butter of our business" is the witty pun used to refer to BreadTalk's research and development team whose sole purpose is to seek new recipes to meet ever-changing tastes of customers. The company replaces 20% of its product range or adds ten new items every quarter to ensure store vitality and excitement for customers every time they visit. The "Haute Bun Couture" aptly promoted by BreadTalk Philippines likens the bakery to a fashion house where new seasons bring forth new styles and refreshing creations. Bread presentation revolves around themes inspired by prevalent social and cultural trends and festivities such as New Years, horoscopes, and national events.

Although BreadTalk's spread of bread items and continuous introduction of new flavors make it a clear leader when it comes to product innovation, the company is aware that competitors, especially small local bakeries, are copying their bestsellers and signature buns, breads, and cakes. But the imitators can never really match the quality and speed that BreadTalk makes its breads and introduces new items. Ultimately true bread lovers return to BreadTalk for the authentic taste and to check out fresh editions of bread items. Besides, the company claims that 70% of its products cannot be found elsewhere, a sure way to elevate the brand value.

However, the company believes that one of its key competitive strengths is the choice of location of retail outlets. All stores are located at strategic and accessible places to capture high human traffic flow. The locations are selected based on the proximity to public transport systems such as bus terminals and train stations, and the composition of the surroundings, such as the presence of departmental stores, cinemas, and supermarkets. Other considerations would be the presence of competition and future development of the area. BreadTalk's strategic locations make it convenient for busy commuters, discerning housewives, and hungry school children to buy their favorite breads which are competitively priced from US 50 cents.

Aside from the tangible assets, excellent service, and successful business strategies, BreadTalk has a simple secret which can be found in its company slogan: "At BreadTalk, we don't just make bread—we make your day." On top of the main ingredients of the finest flour, the purest sugar, and the best yeast, BreadTalk adds in its own personalized "magic" touch of humor, passion, and creativity into the life of its bread.

"Flosss," the cheeky and ever so popular character with ruffled blond top, is BreadTalk's signature bun, a soft, light bread subtly flavored with egg cream and generously covered with pork or chicken floss. "Earthquake Cheese," named by a Taiwanese baker in memory of an earthquake that happened when he was baking, is a cheese-filled loaf with the consistency of brioche. "Crouching Tiger, Hidden Bacon" is an Ang Lee-inspired star in the form of a crusty loaf, rashers of aromatic bacon, and melted cheese hidden inside, plus a dash of black pepper to zest things up. With such a line-up, it is no wonder that a trip to the bakery is an aromatic and self-indulgent delight for both belly and soul.

The widespread market acceptance and apparent ease in which BreadTalk is exporting its home-grown brand to foreign markets might seem surprising to its skeptics. Apart from the usual difficulties of operating in an unfamiliar environment, there is the additional complexity of cross-cultural food products. BreadTalk has proven that the choice of using franchising arrangements is the most feasible for both itself and its partners. The relationship between the company and its foreign franchisees is one which founder George Quek likened to a marriage, a long-term love affair and not a hit-and-run matter.

BreadTalk's flexible and intuitive management enables the company to adapt to changes effectively and yet remain true to its non-traditional approach of elevating bread consumption to a bread culture. Its success at home and in the neighboring countries in ASEAN has encouraged the Singapore premium bakery chain to market its designer bread to the rest of the world.

The expansion of BreadTalk is natural for a typical franchising business. However, its vision to prioritize the ASEAN market as the main target market is something we will elaborate further. The bakery market in ASEAN is growing. Countries such as Indonesia, Thailand, and the Philippines witnessed more than 30% growth rate in their

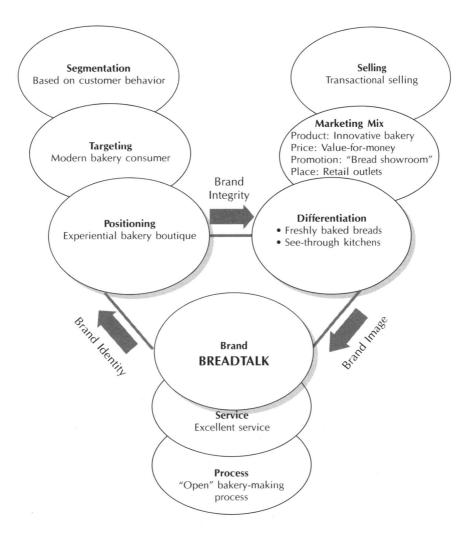

Figure 8.2   Nine core elements of marketing of BreadTalk

bakery industry. BreadTalk's decision to expand into ASEAN is well calculated and timely.

The positioning as an experiential boutique of bakery is appealing for ASEAN consumers who are generally enjoying growing affluence and improved lifestyles. The lifestyle industry is also growing very fast in the region where consumers seek more than product functionality and features. To ASEAN consumers, buying up-market designer breads can be as thrilling as shopping for designer goods. The entire shop design with see-through kitchens, showroom layout, and excellent service is such an attractive and novel concept compared to other bakeries in the region.

BreadTalk has certainly brought a new experience and meaning to the bakery industry here. While the company maintains its key marketing principles and operational standards, it endeavors to localize its breads to suit local tastes and cultures in the different ASEAN countries. Local adjustments are important in a company's regionalization tactics. Without such tactical adjustments, a regional strategy or vision will not work effectively in any host market.

Kijang

Global Going Regional

Being the world's third largest automotive manufacturer, Toyota Motor Corporation (TMC) should be a familiar household name to all. Indeed, many customers today would acquaint stylishness, performance, durability, and safety with any of Toyota's established models found in any country around the world, and this has invariably led to an expansion in their business as they enter into new markets with distinctly different needs. The global brand name has since extended their arms of operations and production in the development of uniquely Asian automobiles to serve the developing nations in the region, the most famous one being the icon of Indonesia—the Toyota Kijang.

The introduction of the Kijang as the national automobile of Indonesia bears testimony to TMC's commitment toward its principle of "in-market production" which seeks to exploit the concept of glorecalization. The parent company was convinced that localized tactics would have to be in play for their success in the various markets, especially when they decided to enter unfamiliar territories. However, they held fast to their responsibility in providing the extensive know-how related to product development, production, and sales through technological transfer with its local partners. PT Toyota Astra Motor (TAM) was henceforth instituted in 1971 in Indonesia as a joint-venture company established by TMC, and the implementation of localized knowledge of the automotive industry gave birth to the first successful model of the Kijang which related well to the needs of Indonesians. Vehicle sales for TAM rose 28% to 59,766 units in the first four months of 2005 compared to the same period the previous year. TAM's market share also increased to 30.6%, up from 29.4% in the same period of 2004. This was the result of the continued domination of its Avanza and Kijang Innova models.

The emergence of the Toyota Kijang is also an ingenious leverage on the change in market forces accelerated by globalization and liberalization of domestic markets. Toward the end of the 20th century, it was clear that Asian countries were beginning to deregulate the automotive market and this was especially vivid in Southeast Asian countries because of the ASEAN Free Trade Area (AFTA) agreement.

The Toyota Kijang is a classic exemplification of TMC's focal shift toward regional strategies and localized tactics. The global power has utilized regional opportunities which stipulated Toyota's joint-venture companies in various Southeast Asian countries to each specialize in the production of different components to increase efficiency. Toyota in Indonesia, for example, specializes in the production of engines; Toyota in Thailand in body press; and Toyota in the Philippines and in Thailand in the production of transmission, steering, gear boxes, and plastic components. Through such a pattern, TMC can more effectively control marketing activities throughout the Asian region, including, among others, in the area of branding.

Generation "Brand"

Constant product development via breakthrough innovations has grown this Indonesian brand name to become what it is today. Their successful reinventions backed by their ability to match the desires of consumers have given them the edge over the competition, and even allowed for TAM's export business to grow in countries which bear similar demographic and economic characteristics as their domestic market. Export business flourished in view of the Kijang's capability of fulfilling the global standard in terms of quality and cost. Countries which have welcomed the Kijang models include India, Brunei Darussalam, Papua New Guinea, and the South Pacific states, amongst others. Kijang engines are also popular in countries like Malaysia, Japan, Taiwan, and the Philippines. To date, TCM has successfully leveraged on the successful initiatives that TAM has pursued with the introduction of the Kijang which is currently the number one selling brand in Indonesia.

The Kijang development cycle has been cited to have gone through five major revamps since 1977, a result of constant innovation and reinvention employed by TAM to continuously meet the needs of their key customers. A total of 762,438 units of Kijang have been sold between 1977 and April 2000. The same period saw five generations of Kijang, each redesigned to better suit the needs of Indonesians. Many locals have since been observed to be abandoning traditional motorcycles as their key modes of transport, and enjoying the prestige of sitting behind their steering wheels with their family safely in tow.

The first generation of Kijang was first launched in 1977. Prior to its debut appearance, the Kijang was already introduced for the first time before the Indonesian public in the 1975 Jakarta Fair as a prototype of Toyota automobiles for the Indonesian market. The introduction of a cheap car was appropriate for the Indonesian markets as the purchasing power of the community at that time allowed the acquisition of no more than basic automobiles with simple facilities.

Back then, the market did not respond positively to the "soap-box-like automobile" of 1977 which lacked the comfort element, and this inevitably paved the way for the second generation series in 1981 which attempted to remove part of the rigidity associated with the initial model. Again, unfavorable reception followed and it soon led TAM to invest in quality market research to access the genuine needs of the locals. The Indonesian community was seen as a class of individuals who needed to rejuvenate their self-respect regardless of their economic status, and material needs like owning a vehicle could perform the magical boost to their esteem and ego.

Extensive research which took center stage during that period drew inspirations from consumers themselves. Ideas and opinions from the Indonesians were strongly encouraged, and they were urged to take on the pivotal role of "designing" their ideal car. TAM organized a contest for the model of a Kijang automobile which could fulfill the conditions of comfort and multiutility. The contest was won by a participant from Central Java and the model drawing was taken to the head office in Japan for the mock-up of the automobile and the manufacturing worthiness was put to test. Three years later, a third-generation Kijang, marked by its trendier model, came into being.

When the third generation was introduced in 1986, it appealed immensely to the crowd as a quality family vehicle which possessed the fundamental elements of comfort and multipurpose which Indonesians saw as key attributes influencing their choice for a vehicle. The new Kijang possessed a more favorable outward appearance and a more attractive car interior with better facilities, including the air conditioner. Locals were also emotionally drawn to the new Kijang as they were convinced that they had contributed to the designing of the model of this generation of the Kijang car. The ownership of the Kijang Rover was so powerful that they saw the need to set up the Rover Club, a club of Kijang Rover owners. This club is akin to that of the very successful Harley Davidson Club in America albeit the scale and scope of this club is much smaller. These initiatives differentiated the Kijang vehicle from the rest, and more importantly, it provided a strong emotional bond with the Indonesian community.

The sweet victory that followed after the successful launch of the third-generation Kijang did not result in complacency. Being at the forefront of the industry, TAM was confident that improved modifications could elevate the status of the Kijang, and provide a boost to its sales volume. The technology of Toyota Original Body, namely a caulking-free vehicle body-making technique, was consequently employed in the fourth generation of the Kijang launched in 1992. This aggressive move allowed TAM to secure its position as *the* family and multipurpose vehicle in the Indonesian market.

In 1997 TAM introduced the fifth generation of Kijang, an automobile manufactured on the basis of the concept of the multicomfort vehicle. This model was made trendier with a rounder appearance and was also designed as a very comfortable vehicle to comply with the concept of a multicomfort vehicle. The fifth-generation Kijang was intended to respond to the development in habits, behavior, and values of its target market as actualized in the ownership and use of Kijang. With this understanding, TAM decided to launch 18 types of Kijang—all with a higher level of comfort—designed for 18 different market niches, from a Kijang which uses diesel oil as fuel right up to the automatic version.

2004 spelt another revolutionary breakthrough for TAM with the launch of the popular Toyota Kijang Innova 2.7V. It was an attempt to expand its already large share of the multipurpose van (MPV) segment. The new vehicle promises to provide more power and convenience to customers and was introduced to fulfill the hopes and expectations of upper-class customers who want an exclusive and luxurious variant of a premium MPV. The sense of luxury is achieved through leather seats and an audio system featuring a six-CD changer and digital music player. It also comes with multi-information display (MID) and audio control placed on a four-spoke steering wheel. The Kijang Innova 2.7V was designed only with automatic transmission and electronic control transmission (ECT) technology, using gate-type shift for easy operation and smooth gear shifts. Safety, comfort, and luxury were all rolled into one to ensure the Kijang's status as Indonesia's favorite car. The Toyota Kijang Innova is the first model the Japanese automaker had manufactured entirely and exclusively outside of Japan. That marked a historic event and a new chapter in the history of Toyota and of the world automobile industry. Their sheer confidence in Indonesia has led Japan's largest automaker to select the country as its global production base for minivans.

A Family Vehicle Is What It Is

TAM was not only committed to product development but saw positioning as another key success factor. Brand building through effective marketing strategies was hence at its core and they wanted to feature the Kijang as a vehicle meant for all family purposes. Surveys of the most popular brand conducted by MarkPlus and *SWA* magazine in 1995 and 1996 for the automotive category proved that Kijang was most popular. The 1996 survey also demonstrated that Kijang was viewed independently of its parent Toyota in that year as Kijang was ranked first, followed by Toyota in the automotive category.

Advertising and promotions were also geared toward portraying the Kijang as a car that was large enough to accommodate the big family and as *the* vehicle that could take the children to school and bring the family for recreational activities. Campaigns of the Kijang could often be spotted splashed across a large number of mediums including newspapers, magazines, television, radio, cinema, billboards, banners, and brochures. TAM also regularly sponsored events such as MTV Asia Awards and Formula One Racing. A highly effective means of promotion was through successful visual displays of their products in malls throughout Jakarta and other major Indonesian cities, which served as their showrooms for the locals to view their exhibits.

In addition, TAM also worked at developing its distribution network and post-sale services through Auto 2000. This expanded its outreach to existing and potential car buyers, and allowed for greater accessibility for loyal Kijang fans. It also elevated its status as a convenient car and one that is easy to care for. With its sales achievement, Kijang is recognized as Indonesia's *de facto* national automobile.

Culturally Different, Kijang Quality Remains

Today, Kijang is not only recognized because of its record sales figures but it is also viewed as a classier vehicle. Automobiles with a higher engine class and a higher price compared with the Kijang like the Opel Blazer and VolksWagon Caravelle have begun to consider the Kijang as their competitor. When exporting to other lucrative markets, TMC is careful not to consistently label the same automobiles with the Kijang tagging which resonates mainly in Indonesia. In Malaysia for instance, the Toyota Unser is in fact a Kijang. In India five versions of the Kijang were introduced, each customized to suit Indian conditions. Local tastes were engineered into the vehicles so as to ensure their suitability for pleasant and safe drives in the various markets they entered. Such tactics also ensured cultural differences were considered in product development which reaffirmed TMC's world-class standards in innovation.

As the pioneering automotive company in Indonesia, TAM has successfully launched the value-for-money Toyota Kijang which serves as a national car simply because it relates so well to the locals. As a powerful brand in its domestic sector, the Kijang is ready to make its way bravely into new markets and take on the challenge of satisfying more drivers in the region. In reality, the Kijang has already been recognized as an ASEAN car especially in relation to the launch of its most recent model, the Toyota Kijang Innova. Adaptation to market changes, innovation, and continuous product development will continue to be its competitive advantage, regardless of where it yearns to venture into in the near future.

Kijang is a sleek family minivan model that commands the "best of both worlds" in Indonesia for its local design and Japanese automobile technology. With its phenomenal success and sustained growth, the Kijang has already made its mark regionally using localized brand names such as Unser in Malaysia and more recently launched as the new-generation innovative international multipurpose vehicle (IMV) under the new brand, Innova.

Localization efforts in the early years sowed the seeds of success for the beloved automobile in Indonesia. With continuous research on customer usage and orientation, Kijang has meticulously fine-tuned its design for the local markets in ASEAN. Its market segmentation

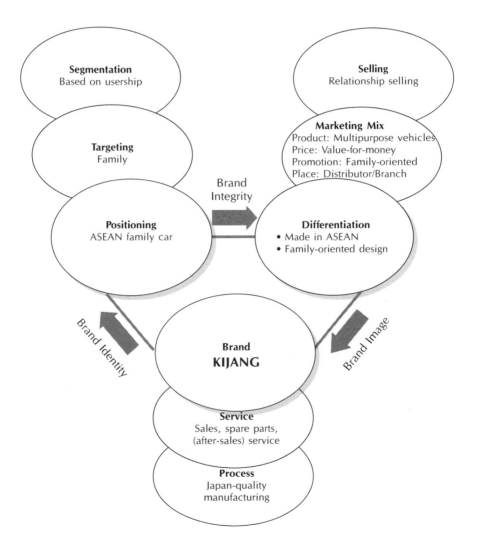

Figure 8.3   Nine core elements of marketing of Kijang

effectively includes the majority of the population with large extended families, thus cementing the brand's offering as a value-for-money vehicle that serves an entire family comfortably.

Lessons Learned

"ASEAN Vision, Local Action" is about your business strategy and implementation tactics. As you envision your plans of expansion outside your home country, you must pay attention to your brand positioning in an ASEAN context and your segmentation and targeting must be consistent for both home and host markets. Building an ASEAN presence entails localization. As commonly said, "One size doesn't fit all." Differentiation, marketing mix, and selling techniques must be customized to suit local conditions and preferences. A regional strategy deployed using local tactics will ensure the creation of a powerful regional brand.

chapter 9

Global Value, ASEAN Strategy, Local Tactic

The world is flat.[1]

Thomas Friedman

In the early days of globalization, there was a distinct difference between a local brand and an imported brand. The local products were usually cheaper and of lower quality but suited the local conditions better. The imported products, particularly from the West, were not just more expensive but were also more problematic due to non-Asian product specifications. One simple example is the toothbrush. Big-sized toothbrushes are clearly not comfortable for the comparatively smaller-built Asians.

When multinational corporations (MNCs) arrived in ASEAN countries to set up factories and sell into the vast consumer market here, they had to rethink their marketing strategies in order to reach out to the local customers. Some learned the hard way and failed. Others took upon themselves to understand the local conditions and requirements, adapted quickly, and prospered.

MNCs must be very careful to create a balance between standardization and local effectiveness. Standardization will increase the efficiencies and consistency in handling global operations. Theodore Levitt, in the 1980s, explained the rationale of global standardization. He described the world as a market where people have the same desires and lifestyles. MNCs, he argued, must forget the idiosyncracies among countries and culture. Instead, they must concentrate on satisfying universal drives.[2] Levitt believed that information technology and

---

[1] Thomas Friedman, *The World Is Flat: A Brief History of the Globalized World in the 21st Century*, Penguin, 2005.

[2] Theodore Levitt, "The Globalization of Markets," *Harvard Business Review*, May–June 1983.

transportation had created a more homogeneous world market. People in the world want the same basic things—things that make their lives easier, increase their time to choose, and increase their purchasing power. As a result, Levitt implied, multinational marketers must realize that substantial economy would be gained through standardization of production, distribution, marketing, and management. Economies of scale would then be translated into higher values to customers by offering higher quality and reliable products at lower prices.

However, as we have seen, with the emergence of regionalization, the global value that the customer receives must not be entirely standardized. There should be a coordinated regional strategy, as each region has different characteristics relative to another. Finally, and importantly, the tactics in each country within each region should also be localized. Therefore, for MNCs focusing on ASEAN, we propose that they adopt the 3C Formula which we called the glorecalization approach.[3]

The first "C" of the glorecalization approach is consistent global value. We argue that the value that a company offers consists of three elements: brand, service, and process.[4] These three elements need to be standardized due to the high costs and investments needed to develop them. A brand that is renowned across the globe can be a great strength for MNCs to enter a particular region. That is why a brand should be standardized in order to have the same brand association, perception, and image everywhere the customers see it. To build such a consistent global brand, MNCs should not rely only on brand building activities. They must also pay attention to the two other value elements that need to be standardized: service and process.

---

[3] The in-depth explanation of the glorecalization approach can be read in Philip Kotler and Hermawan Kartajaya, *Repositioning Asia: From Bubble to Sustainable Economy*, Singapore: John Wiley & Sons, 2000. Glorecalization stands for **G**lobalization-**R**egionalization-**L**ocalization.

[4] For further reading on the elements of Value, see Philip Kotler, Hermawan Kartajaya, Hooi Den Huan, and Sandra Liu, *Rethinking Marketing: Sustainable Market-ing Enterprise in Asia*, Singapore: Pearson Education Asia, 2003.

McDonald's provides a very good example of these two elements. Have you noticed that no matter which McDonald's outlet you visit, it has a very standardized service and process? A clean and comfortable place with friendly service as well as fast delivery can be found in almost every outlet. To achieve this, McDonald's designs its standard operating procedures to be applied to all of its franchising outlets. It even trains its franchisees in Hamburger University to have the same common understanding of how a McDonald's outlet should be managed in terms of its service and process. All three elements of value, namely brand, service, and process, should be standardized at the global level. That is why we call it consistent global value.

The second "C" of the glorecalization approach is coordinated regional strategy. Strategy consists of segmentation, targeting, and positioning.[5] Observe what McDonald's has done. McDonald's in the US may be associated with junk food. In Europe, it is positioned as part of American pop culture. In Asia, its perception as offering mass luxury food vastly differs from perceptions in the US and Europe. The different positioning would definitely require different segmentation and targeting of the market. All three elements of the strategy component, namely segmentation, targeting, and positioning, should be coordinated at the regional level. It means that the strategy in each particular region is the same. That is why we call it coordinated regional strategy.

The third "C" of the glorecalization approach is customized local tactic. Tactic consists of differentiation, marketing mix, and selling.[6] Differentiation is about how you differ yourself from your competitors. It has to be customized at the local level. Then, it should

---

[5] For further reading on the elements of Strategy, see Philip Kotler, Hermawan Kartajaya, Hooi Den Huan, and Sandra Liu, *Rethinking Marketing: Sustainable Market-ing Enterprise in Asia*, Singapore: Pearson Education Asia, 2003.

[6] For further reading on the elements of Tactic, see Philip Kotler, Hermawan Kartajaya, Hooi Den Huan, and Sandra Liu, *Rethinking Marketing: Sustainable Market-ing Enterprise in Asia*, Singapore: Pearson Education Asia, 2003.

be translated into marketing mix and selling techniques, which must also be customized locally.

Although McDonald's has retained its values at the global level, its positioning is different at the regional level. In addition, its tactics are different locally. For example, the McDonald's advertisements in Singapore differ from those in Indonesia or Thailand. More often, the products are localized. Witness the Indonesia-only McSate or Beef Prosperity Burger in Malaysia.

To summarize, there are three "C"s that must be balanced by MNCs eyeing the ASEAN market—consistent global value, coordinated regional strategy, and customized local tactic. This generic approach will be further illustrated by taking the cases of two global brands—Hewlett-Packard and Yamaha.

Hewlett-Packard

The Hewlett-Packard (HP) Story

While Hewlett-Packard may be known for product innovation, the company's corporate development is a tale of reinvention. HP presently provides enterprises and individual consumers a full range of high-tech equipment, including personal computers, servers, storage devices, printers, and networking equipment. Its software portfolio includes operating systems, print management tools, and OpenView, a suite that encompasses application, business, network infrastructure, and product lifecycle management. HP also boasts an IT service organization that is among one of the largest in the world.

The renowned technology champion had its humble beginnings in America. With only US$538, Stanford engineers Bill Hewlett and David Packard started HP in a garage in Palo Alto in California in 1938, under the encouragement of Professor Frederick Terman (considered the founder of Silicon Valley). Hewlett was the idea man while Packard served as the manager. Together, they embarked on their search for good people to join them as they considered human talent a necessity for success. Eventually, business started rolling with the launch of their first product, the audio oscillator.

Sales ballooned from US$34,000 in 1940 to nearly $1 million just three years later. There was strong demand for HP's electronic testing equipment during World War II. HP went public in 1957 and in 1959, subsequently expanded beyond the US by establishing a marketing organization in Switzerland and a manufacturing plant in West Germany. From then on, HP has never looked back. Global establishments were set up in various countries all over the world, and today, it stands as a true global conglomerate. Specifically, HP's operations in Asia and especially in ASEAN have also grown in number, signaling the rewards of its regional strategies.

Consistent Global Value: The HP Way

The HP Way, the title of a memoir written by David Packard, espouses the virtues of consensus building and long-term planning. The legendary corporate culture that valued teamwork and cared for employees had always been the beacon of the company's operations and HP was not seen to create a product unless it represented a "technical contribution." The principles and philosophies behind this companywide culture also brought about a paternalistic way of using generous health and retirement benefits to foster employee loyalty.

In recent years, however, the HP Way has been synonymous with stodginess, and corporate reinvention through streamlining strategies was put in place because HP was competing in an industry where product cycles are sometimes measured in months, not years. By simplifying operations and management as well as cutting costs and getting managers focused on the urgent issues, HP is confident of a bigger and brighter future. It will not resist change and is set to sit out of the comfort zone and achieve the status of a market leader.

In terms of process, benchmarking with the industry's best performers will persist to allow constant innovation to dominate HP's daily operations. Change will continually be viewed as an opportunity to grow and expand into new areas that build on HP's technologies, competencies, and customer interests.

Diversity and inclusion will continue to be the key drivers of creativity, innovation, and invention. Putting differences to work and connecting everyone to the power of technology in the marketplace, workplace, and community will continue to be HP's winning formula. A leaner corporation is underway, as HP works at shedding bulky cost structures and eliminating impediments of the past which have posed as competitive disadvantages to HP as compared to its competitors.

Aggressive Regional Marketing

HP established a presence in the Asia Pacific in 1963 when the first office was set up in Japan. Today, the corporation has more than 26,000 employees in this region with operations in 14 countries—Australia, China, Hong Kong, India, Indonesia, Japan, Korea, Malaysia, New Zealand, the Philippines, Singapore, Taiwan, Thailand, and Vietnam. It has a special team encompassing the Southeast Asian countries/ Taiwan internally labeled as SEAT.

A network of 20 solution centers provide enterprise customers and partners here with an avenue to test, benchmark, and carry out proof of concepts on proposed solutions. These centers provide drirect and remote access to a full range of HP hardware, software, and engineering skills, offering a first-hand experience of how infrastructure and partner solutions work together. In addition, there are 158 customer service centers in the Asia Pacific, providing warranty and after-sales support of HP technologies.

To provide for HP's global market, 12 manufacturing centers were established in Australia, China, India, Japan, Malaysia, Singapore, and Thailand. These facilities manufacture desktop PCs, notebooks, pocket PCs, workstations, servers, storage, networking products, printers, scanners, inkjet cartridges, and inks.

HP conducts extensive R&D out of China, Singapore, India, and Japan for products that are marketed both regionally and globally in the areas of networking products, software and mobile, general office, and wide-format printing categories. Its Indian labs in Bangalore were set up to create world-class research labs, focusing on the needs of emerging markets by understanding relevant social, cultural, economic, and technological drivers of specific countries and regions. Research is focused on language technology; low-cost Internet and computing access devices; communication concepts and techniques for developing countries; and new models for human interaction with IT equipment and software.

In April 2006, HP opened an Asia Pacific IP (intellectual property) Licensing Center in Singapore to serve the fast-growing Asia-Pacific market. The center will provide companies, governments, research institutes, and universities in the region access to HP's technology and IP through licensing agreements. Licenses are available for HP's know-how, patents, trademarks, and copyrights in a broad range of technology areas, from its IP portfolio which includes more than 30,000 patents. This function extends HP's worldwide IP licensing program which was formed in 2003 as a means of generating additional value from HP's IP by increasing its use in new markets through licenses to third parties.

The second case shows how a widely recognized brand, Yamaha, has applied the Glorecalization approach fruitfully in its ASEAN market where it has skillfully adopted a regional strategy and localized approach while protecting its global brand.

Yamaha

The founding of Yamaha, the well-known Japanese manufacturer of musical instruments, over 100 years ago, started what is known as *Kando*. *Kando* is a Japanese word that symbolizes the simultaneous feelings of deep satisfaction and intense excitement that people experience when they encounter something of exceptional value. *Kando* has made Yamaha one of the best-loved music companies in the world. It has also made the 50-year-old Yamaha Motor one of the leaders in the motorcycle industry. This case will discuss the Glorecalization approach (Globalization of Value, Regionalization of Strategy, and Localization of Tactic) in Yamaha Motor that is implemented in its target markets. It will explore the global value that Yamaha applies all over the world, the strategy in each region especially ASEAN, and the localized tactic in each ASEAN country.

The Power of Glorecalization

A multinational company (MNC) has its own complexity in managing its operations worldwide. Not only must it standardize its global value and adapt its tactic locally, but it also needs to adapt its strategy at the regional level. Yamaha Motor as an MNC faces this challenge. Yamaha Motor's value must be maintained consistent globally, yet the strategy must be coordinated at the regional level, while the tactic must be customized locally. Therefore, an MNC focusing on several regions like Yamaha Motor must apply the glorecalization approach. According to this approach, an MNC with regional focus must have the 3C formula: consistent global value, coordinated regional strategy, and customized local tactic. The approach itself is proven to be very successfully implemented in Yamaha Motor.

Yamaha's Global Standard

Despite the fact that Yamaha is a Japanese company, the Yamaha name has become a globally recognized brand. Thanks to the patronage of music lovers, the Yamaha brand has become very strong throughout three centuries—the 19th, the 20th, and the 21st. The name Yamaha is rooted in the name of its founder, Torakusu Yamaha. Familiar with Western science and technology from his youth, Yamaha initially found employment repairing medical equipment. This led to a request to repair an organ, a project that resulted in the birth of the Yamaha brand. Confident of the potential of his business, Yamaha struggled against great odds to establish Yamaha Organ Works. Entrepreneurial spirit, far-sightedness, and determination to overcome difficulties fueled his passion to succeed. It was the spirit of creating *Kando*. This same spirit formed the foundation of the Yamaha brand, and is a vital legacy of Yamaha Corporation. Today, Yamaha is a leader in businesses ranging from musical instruments and audiovisual products to information technology products, new media services, home furnishings, specialty metals, music education, and resort facilities.

In the last 50 years of its existence the brand made inroads into the motorcycle industry by setting up Yamaha Motor. Although the characteristics of the motorcycle industry are very dissimilar than those of music, the brand is evidently able to be transferred to that industry. *Kando* signifies the joy of music that Yamaha brings to everyone around the globe. After achieving remarkable success in spreading *Kando* to music fans, Yamaha has also succeeded in conveying *Kando* to motorcycle riders.

Ever since its founding as a motorcycle manufacturer in 1955, Yamaha Motor has pledged to give the world the best-quality motorcycles that contribute to the quality of life. Its operations now cover the three biggest and the most promising market for motorcycles—ASEAN, the US, and Europe. Although the strategy in each of these regions is different, the brand of Yamaha is maintained the same. The Yamaha brand, along with its brand slogan "Touching Your Heart" is applied in every corner of the globe. In addition, the brand identity, the "Three Tuning Forks" mark together with the Yamaha logo, is used all over the world. This identity originally represents the three essential musical elements: melody, harmony, and rhythm. However, it also symbolizes the cooperative relationship that links the three pillars of its business: Technology, Production, and Sales.

Two of the pillars—Technology and Production—support Yamaha in creating value to its customers. Yamaha enhances its value to its customers by creating the motorcycles they need. To enable Yamaha to do this, it has developed a strong process of value creation. Yamaha builds superior research and development (R&D) capabilities in technology, continuously creating innovative products. World-class production processes are also implemented. These main processes of value creation are maintained at the global level and remain the same in every Yamaha manufacturing facility.

Yamaha's ASEAN Perspective

Although value creation is maintained at a consistent global level, strategy is differentiated at the regional level. It means that the strategy in ASEAN is different than that in the US and in Europe. The segmentation and targeting are done by region. The positioning is adjusted to the target segment in a particular region.

There are three cornerstones of Yamaha's strategy—growth, profitability, and value. Growth is the foundation for the strategy in ASEAN, while profitability is the foundation for the strategy in the US and Europe. ASEAN is the market with strong growth in the motorcycle industry. That is why Yamaha is enhancing its business growth in this market. The US and Europe also form a big market but their growth is much smaller than that of ASEAN. That is why Yamaha is only maximizing its profitability there. Although the foundation is different, all three regions share the third cornerstone, value. No matter what market it is, customer value is still the main focus. It must remain as the global standard.

Because the foundation of the strategy is different, the positioning in each region is also different. In the US, the Yamaha motorcycle is positioned as the customized motorcycle in terms of accessories. The product comes out as the Star series. The slogan for the product series is "We Build the Bike, You Make It Yours." The slogan means customers are allowed to customize their own motorcycles using the Star Custom Accessories. This strategy is based on the fact that Americans love to decide what their motorcycles should look like, just like Harley Davidson owners. Yamaha called the strategy the Star Strategy.

The positioning in Europe is also different. Although the foundation of strategy in Europe is similar to that in the US, the positioning of Yamaha there is quite different. In Europe, Yamaha is positioned as the producer of the best manual transmission (MT) motorcycles in the world. The product comes out as the MT series. That is why Yamaha called the strategy in Europe the MT Strategy.

In ASEAN, the Yamaha brand is positioned very differently. In ASEAN, Yamaha is positioned as the producer of stylish, sporty, and innovative motorcycles with its series of four-stroke and automatic models. This strategy is called the ABC Strategy. As the US and European markets mature, the ASEAN market is becoming more promising for Yamaha. The forecasted demand in the three ASEAN markets alone (Indonesia, Thailand, and Vietnam) is much more than the demand in the US and European markets combined.

Aggressive action has been taken to capture the market. Yamaha aggressively launched the new four-stroke automatic and high-value-added models while further enhancing the positioning of the sporty motorcycles, especially to youngsters. The new sporty four-stroke model like Jupiter-Z (110 cc motorcycle) and recently launched Jupiter-MX (135 cc) are positioned to be the flagship products of Yamaha in the ASEAN region. In addition, the more popular automatic models such as the Nouvo and Mio complement the wide range of Yamaha motorcycle sporty models.

Yamaha has also strengthened its sales network by building flagship shops in three main ASEAN target markets—Indonesia, Thailand, and Vietnam. Moreover, Yamaha has planned to boost its production capacity by establishing the second plant in Indonesia and the parts casting plant in Vietnam. These plants will serve the entire ASEAN region and the motorcycles manufactured will be specifically positioned as ASEAN motorcycles.

One of the most popular promotions of these ASEAN motorcycles is the one that was recently conducted for the Jupiter-MX. The Jupiter-MX model is the new model that is being promoted all over ASEAN. Yamaha conducted the PAN-ASEAN tour using this type of motorcycle. The tour was done in six major ASEAN countries—Indonesia, Thailand, Vietnam, Malaysia, Philippines, and Singapore. There are two main reasons why the tour was done in ASEAN countries. The first one is because the Jupiter-MX is positioned as the new 135 cc ASEAN motorcycle and will be marketed in the ASEAN region. The second one is to test its endurance and its performance in terms of speed. The motorcycle is also being positioned as the most durable motorcycle in the region.

Yamaha's Local Action

The Yamaha global value and regional strategy will not be successful if the marketing tactic is not localized for each country. That is why in each country in a particular region, Yamaha acts local.

At the country level in ASEAN, Yamaha has very dissimilar differentiation to support its positioning. The differentiation is customized according to local customs and behavioral patterns. Although the product quality is the same, the differentiation that is being emphasized is different. In Indonesia and Malaysia, the differentiations are the motorcycle's speed and engine performance as well as its durability and economic fuel consumption. In Thailand, the economic fuel consumption, durability, and comfort are emphasized more. In Vietnam, the exclusive image and status symbol perception associated with the motorcycle complement its differentiation in economic fuel consumption, durability, and comfort.

The differentiation is then translated into customized marketing mix. In Indonesia and Malaysia, Yamaha offers the two-stroke and four-stroke motorcycles, while in Thailand and Vietnam, it offers the four-stroke and automatic models. The pricing of these products is also customized to local preference and affordability.

For every major ASEAN country, Yamaha applies different taglines for its marketing communications. In Thailand, it uses the tagline "Switch Your Life." In Indonesia, it uses *"Selalu Terdepan"* ("Always in Front"). "Powers Your Passion" is used in Malaysia while *"Hai Song Khac"* ("To Live Your Own Way")is used in Vietnam. In Thailand and Vietnam, the promotion is represented by F4 (a well-known Taiwanese singer group). In Indonesia, Yamaha has DEWA (a famous Indonesian band) promoting its products.

Conclusion

The global standard, regional perspective, and local action of Yamaha have made Yamaha one of the strongest motorcycle manufacturers globally. Yamaha understands the importance of having consistent value creation across the globe while having coordinated regional strategy across the region, and customized local tactic in each host country. It is this Glorecalization approach that made Yamaha a *Kando*-creating company not only in the music industry but also in the motorcycle industry.

Lessons Learned

The glorecalization approach is a simple yet powerful model to create successful global brands in regional markets. The 3C formula (consistent global value, coordinated regional strategy, and customized local tactic) is the core essence of this approach. To win customers and capture market share in any regional market, it is imperative to follow the 3Cs closely. As we have demonstrated in the case studies for HP and Yamaha, successful regional marketing in ASEAN is derived by simply applying a consistent global value while implementing ASEAN regional-level strategies and local-level tactics.

Index

Abacus International, 101
AEC (ASEAN Economic
    Community), ix, 47, 48
AFTA (ASEAN Free Trade Area),
    37, 45, 165
AIA (ASEAN Investment Area), 45
AICO (ASEAN Industrial
    Cooperation Scheme), 45
AIMST (Asian Institute of
    Medicine, Science and
    Technology), 99
AirAsia, vii, 152–158
Airbus, 153, 155
Akamatsu, Kaname, 2, 42
analog systems, 13, 17, 20
Ang, Ramon S., 122
APEC (Asia-Pacific Economic
    Cooperation), 36, 46
Apple Computer, 145
ARF (ASEAN Regional Forum),
    44, 47
ASC (ASEAN Security
    Community), ix, 44, 47, 48
ASCC (ASEAN Socio-Cultural
    Community), ix, 47, 48
ASEAN
    attraction for multinationals,
        133–134
    brief history of, 39–40
    business landscape of, viii, 37,
        38, 46, 49–55
    consumer market size, ix, x, 5,
        46, 71, 72
    digital challenges for, 15–24

economic performance, v, 45, 56
    factors determining growth of,
        40–41
    major industries, exports, and
        imports, 57–59
    major investors in, 35, 39, 64
    need for regional integration,
        vii, viii, ix, 2, 37, 38, 60
    organizational structure, 43, 44
ASEAN Community 2015, viii, ix,
    45, 48, 51, 52
ASEAN customer, 72–76
ASEAN Declaration, 37, 47
ASEAN Information Infrastructure,
    15
ASEAN Summit, 43, 44, 48
ASEAN-5, 43, 56
ASEAN-6, 68
ASEM (Asia-Europe Meeting), 46
Asian financial crisis, vii, viii, 3,
    20, 27, 32–33, 34, 40, 43,
    49, 70, 91, 128
Asian miracle, 3, 36, 42, 43
ASME (Association of Small and
    Medium Enterprises), 88,
    160, 163

bakery boutique, vii, 80, 159
Bangkok Heart Institute, 102
Bangkok Hospital, 101–105
Bangkok International Hospital, 103
Bangkok Neurological Gamma
    Center, 102
Bengawan Solo, 86–89

Bidaya, Thanong, 128
Bintang Toedjoe, 114, 115
Black Canyon, vii, 128–132
BookWeb, 140, 141
bottled tonic drinks, 107–111
brand building, 84, 133, 149–
    150, 174
brand value, 149, 151
Branson, Richard, 152
BreadTalk, vii, 80, 159–164
budget carrier, 153
budget terminal, 154
Budimas Charitable Foundation,
    99
Butterfly Effect, 25

cake redemption voucher, 87
Carrefour, 69
CEPT (Common Effective
    Preferential Tariff) scheme,
    45, 68
cerveza, 120
change
    forces of, 6–9
    brought about by globalization,
        26, 27, 28
    horizontal stream, 7, 8
    in retail banking trends, 72
    S stream, 8, 9
    as a value migrator, 53, 67
    vertical stream, 8
Chevron, 29
Chitnarapong, Pravit, 128
clove cigarette. *See kretek*
CNOOC (China National
    Offshore Oil Corporation),
    29
Coca-Cola, 105, 106, 108

Cold War, 29
company mission, 83, 84
competency, 78
competition, v, vi, 9, 14, 38, 43,
    45, 52, 66, 67, 68–69, 70
Comyns, 118
Creative Technology, 70

Dawar, Niraj, 69
de Ycaza, Don Enrique Maria
    Barretto, 120
demand-driven market, 78
Deng Xiao Ping, 31
differentiation, 71, 83, 85, 149, 175
digital convergence, 144, 146
digital divide, 12, 14, 15, 16, 19
digital technology, 13
discount airline, 152
Dji Sam Soe, 90–94
Dubai Ports World, 29

EALAF (East Asia-Latin America
    Forum), 46
e-ASEAN Business Council, 19
e-ASEAN Framework Agreement,
    15, 19, 23
e-commerce, 15, 19, 23
e-government, 19, 21, 22
EPRG company orientations,
    78–79
Es Teller 77, vii, 80
e-society, 19
ethnocentric companies, 79
Eu Kong, 124
Eu Yan Sang, 124–128
Eu, Richard, 126
eugenol, 190
European Union, 36, 44, 46, 51

experiential shopping, 140, 147
Extra Joss, 113–116

fast-moving consumer goods, 5,
    110
FDI (foreign direct investment),
    34, 35, 39, 50, 51, 56, 64
Fernandes, Tony, 152, 153, 157
flying geese formation, 2, 3, 42,
    43, 56, 57, 133
4 Cs, 6, 77
4C Diamond sub-model, 6

Franchising, 95, 131, 160, 162
Friedman, Thomas L., 9, 173
Frost, Tony, 69
full-cost carriers, 152, 157

gamma knife technology, 102
Gandhi, Rajiv, 32
geocentric companies, 79
global integration, 19, 27, 28, 56,
    68, 70
globalization
    and challenges for ASEAN, 3,
        38–41
    effects of, 25–26, 27
    history of, 28–30
    problems of, 28, 32, 33
    vs. regionalization, 35–37
Globe Telecom, 96
glorecalization, 71, 165, 174, 175
Goldilocks, 94–97
Goldstar, 144
greenfield investment, 34, 50
Grove, Andy, 66

Hanusz, Mark, 93
heart share, 92, 151

Hewlett, Bill, 176
Hewlett-Packard, 176–179
HSBC, 80

IBM, 123
ICT (information and
    communication
    technologies), 14–19
    impact on economy, 22–24
ICT capacity, 19
ICT marketplace, 19
ICT strategies in ASEAN, 19–22
IMF (International Monetary
    Fund), 32, 33
Industrial Revolution, 23
infostate, 15, 16, 18, 20, 74, 75
integrative healthcare, 126
integrative medicine centers, 125
Intel Corporation, 66
Interbrand, 143, 149
International Hospital Federation,
    104
Internet, the, 11, 13, 15, 25, 29,
    31, 139, 140, 155
intra-ASEAN trade, 62, 68

J. Boag & Son, 122
JAMA (Japan Automobile
    Manufacturers Association),
    64
jamu, 113, 114
JetStar, 156
Johns Hopkins International, 104
just-in-time production and
    delivery, 88

Kando, 180, 181
Kijang, 164–172
Kinokuniya, 139–142

Kirin Brewery Company, 122
Koeda, Itaru, 64
kretek, 90, 92, 93

Lee, Byung-Chull, 144
Lee, Kun-Hee, 144
Lenovo, 23
Levitt, Theodore, 71, 173, 174
Liem Seeng Tee, 90
Liew, Anastasia, 86
Lim Chong Yah, 35, 66
Linux, 26
localization, 71, 151, 172
Lorenz, Edward N., 25
low-cost carriers, vii, 153

Magnussen, Erik, 118
Malaysia Stock Exchange, 153
marketing mix, 71, 149, 175
Maslow's hierarchy of needs, 73
mass customization, 14
MasterCard International, 97
MBF Cards, 97–100
MBF Holdings Berhad, 97
McDonald's, 76, 159, 175
medical tourism, 101
metalesce, 118
meta-needs, 73
MNC (multinational
    corporation), 65, 180
Mohamad, Mahathir, 152, 153
Munro, Nick, 118

NAFTA (North American Free
    Trade Agreement), 37, 56
niche cards, 98, 100
niche marketing, 98, 100, 112
nine core elements of strategic
    business triangle, 149–150

Nokia, 145
Number One Tonic Drink,
    105–111

OECD (Organization for
    Economic Co-operation and
    Development), 23
Ogilvy and Mather Singapore, 75
open-door policy, 31, 106
Options Information Company,
    104
Orbicom (International Network
    of UNESCO Chairs in
    Communications), 15

P&O, 29
Packard, David, 176
Pepsi, 105, 106, 108
Perlmutter, Howard V., 78
Pewter, 117–120
Pho24, vii
Pink, Daniel, 73
Pinoy, 68, 94, 96, 97
polycentric companies, 79
positioning, 52, 71, 83, 85, 89,
    149, 151, 175
positioning-differentiation-brand
    triangle, 55, 71, 83, 84, 89,
    94, 97, 100, 105, 111, 116,
    120, 124, 128, 131, 138,
    139, 142, 146, 149
Private Hospital Association of
    Thailand, 104
PT AWAIR, 154
PT Toyota Astra Motor, 165

Quek, George, 159, 162

regiocentric companies, 79

regionalization, vii, ix, x, 2, 4, 35, 36, 38, 57, 65, 68, 70, 74, 81
risk attitude, 6, 53, 77, 78
Royal Selangor, 117–120
Rugman, Alan, 35, 36, 79, 133

Saatchi & Saatchi Vietnam, 109
Sampoerna, 90, 91, 92, 93
Samsung, 143–146
San Miguel, vii, 120–124
Sanyo, 144
SARS, 33, 127
segmentation, 71, 72, 76, 149, 175
Selberan, 118
Shin Corporation, 29, 153
Shinawatra, Thaksin, 29
Singapore Press Holdings, 160
sinseh, 124
Siva, Karthik, 74
smoking statistics, Indonesia, 91
SMS booking of air flights, 155
Sony, 143, 144, 145
standardization, 70, 71, 151, 173
strategic business triangle, 71, 84, 89, 116, 127, 132, 134, 138, 142, 149, 151
stretch possibility, 61, 53, 77
STV (Strategy-tactic-value triangle), 149, 151. *See also* positioning-differentiation-brand triangle
Summa Foundation, 104
Superbrands International, 104
supply-driven market, 77
Sustainable Model, 38

Tan Hiep Phat Company, 106
TCM (traditional Chinese medicine), 124–127
technology
    as a force of change, 6–9
    as key growth driver, 14
Temasek Holdings, 29
Terman, Frederick, 176
Tesco, 69
3C formula, 71, 174–176, 180, 185
3G technology, 14
3M, 134–138
Tiger Airways, 156
top-of-mind awareness, 95
Toshiba, 144
Toyota Motor Corporation, 70, 164
Transferability, 132
Triple C theory, 35
Tune Air Sdn. Bhd., 152

UNCTAD (UN Conference on Trade and Development), 34, 50
UNDP (United Nations Development Program), 44, 46, 50
United Nations, 29
Unocal, 29, 32
UTAR (Universiti Tunku Abdul Rahman), 99

value creation, 92, 181
value demander, 6, 53, 77
value migrator, 6, 53, 77
value supplier, 6, 53, 77

Valueair, 156
VAP (Vientiane Action Program),
     48
Virgin Records, 152
Visa International, 97

Warner Music Group, 152
Wen Jiabao, 51
WHO (World Health
     Organization), 33
Wimbledon Effect, 29

winning value application, 78
WTO (World Trade
     Organization), 2, 31, 35

Y2K, 32
Yamaha, 179–184
Yamaha Motor, 179, 180, 181
Yamaha, Torakusu, 180
yin-yang, 124
Yong Koon, 117